The Pioneers

Darlene Irvin Parsons

McClain Printing Company
Parsons, West Virginia 26287
2007

International Standard Book Number 0-87012-762-4
Library of Congress Control Number 2007903106
Printed in the United States of America
Copyright © 2007 by Darlene Irvin Parsons
Parsons, West Virginia
All Rights Reserved
2007

Printed by
McClain Printing Company
Parsons, WV
www.mcclainprinting.com

Dedication

The Parsonses were a spirited lot
United by deep morals and convictions
Dedicated to God and family
Home and country

They forged a new frontier
Fought the Indians
Suffered, as friends and neighbors died

Divided by political views
Separated by a Civil War
Undaunted
They prevailed

A new country
A new county
A new state

This book is dedicated to
The honored men and women of

The Parsons Family

CONTENTS

Chapter I.
William Parsons- - - - - - - - - - Page 1

Chapter II.
Thomas Parsons Sr. - - - - - - - -Page 2
Parsonses in Hampshire County
Thomas Parsons' Estate
Will of Thomas Parsons Sr.

Chapter III.
Thomas Parsons Jr. - - - - - - - - Page 7
Parsonses in Hardy County
Isaac Parsons~Tucker County's First School
Thomas Parsons and Robert Maxwell
Will of Thomas Parsons Jr.

Chapter IV.
William Parsons- - - - - - - - - - Page 16
William Parsons in Randolph County, Virginia
Will of William Parsons
Tucker County Census 1860
Parsonses in Tucker County
Virginia (Parsons) McCabe
Job Ward Parsons
Adonijah B. Parsons
James Parsons

CONTENTS

Chapter V.
Squire Job Parsons Sr. - - - - - - - - - - - - Page 47
Hannahsville Skirmish
Lieutenant Robert A. McChesney, C.S.A.
Job Parsons Taken Prisoner
Rebecca (Parsons) Rummell Bonnifield

Chapter VI.
Captain James Parsons - - - - - - - - Page 59
French and Indian War 1754-1763
Forts in Hardy County
The Battle of the Trough
Lord Dunmore's War 1774
Hardy County
Moorefield
South Branch Manor
Hardy County Cattle Commerce
Slaves of the Parsons Brothers
Tucker County Indians
Captain Parsons Discovers Tucker County
First White Men in Tucker County
John Minear
Fort Minear
Bernard Sims Murdered
Jonathan Minear Murdered
Minear, Cooper and Cameron Murdered
Will of Captain James Parsons
The Captain James Parsons House
James Parsons to John Smith Deed 1809

CONTENTS

Chapter VII.
Solomon Parsons, M.D. - - - - - - - - - - **Page 96**
Hannah (Parsons) Parsons
Diana (Parsons) Parsons
Parsonsville Passes Into County History
John Rust Parsons
Formation of Tucker County
Tucker County Elections
First County Officials
Tucker County Courthouse War
Delegate Solomon Parsons
West Virginia Statehood
Virginia Secedes
Clarksburg Convention
First Wheeling Convention
Second Wheeling Convention - First Session
Reorganized Government - General Assembly of Virginia
Second Wheeling Convention - Second Session
West Virginia Constitutional Convention
Civil War~Imboden in Tucker County
Brigadier General John Daniel Imboden, C.S.A.
St. George and Holly Meadows Churches
First Parsons Family Reunion 1907
Church Lease 1844
Church Deed 1868
Will of Solomon Parsons

CONTENTS

Chapter VIII.
James William Parsons - - - - - - - - - - - - -**Page 200**
Sansome Elliott Parsons
Will of Ann Eliza (Prentis) Parsons

Chapter IX.
Solomon John Parsons - - - - - - - - - - - - - **Page 206**
Emma (Parsons) Parsons
James W. Parsons to Solomon J. Parsons Deed 1873
Descendants of Solomon and Emma Parsons
William Parsons Hahn
Olive Marie (Hahn) Lipscomb
Will of Solomon John Parsons
Will of Emma (Parsons) Parsons
St. George, West Virginia
St. George Academy

Chapter X.
Worley Parsons - - - - - - - - - - - - - - - -**Page 225**
Senior Citizen Worley Parsons
Eva (Metz) Parsons
St. George United Methodist Women
Devoted Parsons Women
James Everett Parsons
Hattie (Oaster) Parsons
Solomon John Parsons House

ACKNOWLEDGMENTS

Melinda Sherman Parsons
Donna Jean Schoonover
Diana Irvin Helms
Kevin G. White
Marvin E. Parsons
Alice Parsons Phillips
St. George United Methodist Church
Gladys Jane Pifer
Judith A. Parsons
Mary Parsons Gordon
Barbara Gutshall Roy
Judy Greek
Darla J. Stemple
Ruth Bohon
Betty Metz

I am also especially grateful to those who have inspired me.

INTRODUCTION

From the onset, I need to clarify that this text is not an attempt at Parsons Family genealogy. It is a solitary effort created for the sake of posterity. My intention is to provide a record of the Parsonses who came to this country from England and settled in the eastern panhandle of West Virginia, which at that time was Spotsylvania County, Virginia. Members of this branch of the family migrated to what eventually became known as Tucker County, West Virginia.

The story begins with Thomas Parsons Sr. and progresses to Worley Parsons who descended from two of Parsons' sons. Worley's mother, Emma Parsons, descended from the eldest son, Thomas Parsons Jr. Worley's father, Solomon John Parsons, descended from the second son, Captain James Parsons. As I relay the story of this illustrious family, you will accompany them on their journey through Hampshire, Hardy, Randolph and Tucker counties. This includes their involvement in Indian wars, Revolutionary and Civil wars that occurred during their lifetime.

When Thomas B. Rummell, a young attorney from Beverly, Virginia, compiled the first census of Tucker County in 1860, there were three magisterial districts of Hannahsville, St. George and Black Fork. Residing within the districts were 245 families, and 16 of those families were Parsonses. Even though some were indirectly related to Worley Parsons, each had descended from Thomas Parsons Sr. Several of those Parsonses contributed significantly to Tucker County history; therefore, they have been integrated within this narrative.

This account also includes the fascinating adventures of two frontiersmen, the Parsons brothers. It relates their encounters with the Indians and the discovery of the beautiful Horseshoe lands and Cheat River valley. According to most sources, Captain James

Parsons is believed to be one of the first white men to enter Tucker County.

Job Parsons Sr. was a Confederate sympathizer, and Dr. Solomon Parsons was a Unionist. Each carved a stone in Tucker County's Civil War era. Dr. Parsons proved essential in the formation of Tucker County from Randolph County. He also served as a delegate to the Second Wheeling Convention, whose sole purpose was to create the new state of West Virginia. Solomon's son, James W. Parsons, represented Tucker County as a delegate to the West Virginia Constitutional Convention.

The story wanes with Solomon John Parsons, a prominent farmer in the St. George area, who built a farmhouse (circa 1891) on land pre-empted by his father. The homestead has remained in the Parsons family for over one hundred years.

This text includes many recurring names: Thomas, James, William, Solomon and Isaac. These names have been favorites of the Parsonses throughout their history and may cause difficulty for the reader. It tends to become even more confusing when *Parsonses* married *Parsonses*. I have kept this in mind as I wrote this account and have done my best to lessen the confusion.

Dates need to be clarified in this book as well. Tucker County was part of Randolph County, Virginia, for sixty-nine years. When the early Parsonses migrated to western Virginia, it was indeed Randolph County, Virginia. Tucker County was not established until 1856. West Virginia was part of Virginia until 1863.

Information gathered here is possible with the labor of noted historians of Tucker, Randolph, Hardy and Hampshire counties. Without the effort of these renowned scholars, this undertaking would not have been possible.

Two historians who included much of the Parsons family history in their work are Hu Maxwell and Homer Floyd Fansler. Maxwell's

History of Tucker County (1884) was written shortly after the period in which much of the Parsons story takes place. He wrote the first Tucker County history at twenty-four years of age. Homer Floyd Fansler's *History of Tucker County West Virginia* (1962) was written when Fansler was sixty-two years of age. Fansler had served in both world wars and had written over one hundred procedural bulletins while serving his country. Shortly after the publication of his history, he left Tucker County. Fansler died January 15, 1965, in the veterans hospital in Lake City, Florida, and is buried in the Andersonville National Cemetery, Andersonville, Georgia.

Virginia Parsons MacCabe's *Parsons Family History and Record* (1913) provided an essential reference to early Parsons ancestry. MacCabe's record was published when she was sixty-four years of age and has been the single account of Parsons genealogy for nearly one hundred years.

We are extremely fortunate that Parsons family events occurring in the 1700s to early 1900s are permanently recorded in our state and county histories. The Parsonses are a vital family who made their mark on countless pages. It is my desire that these men and women be distinguished for their character, political and spiritual beliefs. My wish is that the founding fathers of the Parsons Family be remembered for the impact they had in settling Tucker County, West Virginia.

Darlene Irvin Parsons
Parsons, West Virginia
2007

Chapter I

WILLIAM PARSONS

Parsons family history began in England in the year 1400. There, lived a man named John Parr who had twelve sons. As his sons grew to manhood, they became known as *Parr's sons*. The name was spelled Parrssons until eventually some of the middle letters were dropped, leaving the name of today. (MacCabe 7)

In early colonial days, two brothers by the name of Parsons, descendants of the original John Parr, came to America. One established himself in New England, near Boston, and the other settled in Virginia. (MacCabe 7)

It is the Virginia branch of the Parsons family from which this story evolves, beginning with Thomas Parsons Sr., son of William Parsons, who settled on the eastern shore of Maryland in 1725. Virginia Parsons MacCabe wrote, "...it is absolutely certain this William Parsons is a descendant of the Parsons brothers who came from England to America (in) 1635." (18)

Chapter II

THOMAS PARSONS SR.

Thomas Parsons Sr. and Parthenia (Baldwin) Parsons

Married: About 1729

Seven children: Thomas Jr., James, Isaac, Prudence (Parsons) Cunningham, Arness (Parsons) Welton, Baldwin, and Elizabeth (Parsons) Heinsman

Thomas Parsons Sr. Born about 1688, Philadelphia, Pennsylvania Died about May 27, 1771, Hampshire County, Virginia

Parthenia Baldwin: Born about 1697, Bucks County, Pennsylvania
(Genealogical Society of Utah)
(Some sources state born in Hampshire County, Virginia)
Died (unknown), Hampshire County, Virginia

Thomas Parsons Sr. is the maternal great-great-great-grandfather of Worley Parsons who was a lifelong resident of St. George, West Virginia.

PARSONSES IN HAMPSHIRE COUNTY

MacCabe tells us that Thomas Parsons Sr. and sons settled in Hampshire County, Virginia, in 1700. (Preface) The origin of many West Virginia counties began with the formation of Spotsylvania County, Virginia. This area was formed from Essex, King William and King and Queen counties in 1721.

Orange County was created from Spotsylvania County in 1734 and consisted of all the territory west of the Blue Ridge. In November 1738, this area was divided into the two counties of Augusta and Frederick. Augusta was formed in 1738, but county government was not organized until 1745. Frederick was established in 1743.

Augusta County, Virginia, at one time, comprised the southern part of the Valley of Virginia and all the vast territory of Virginia west of the Valley, with Staunton as its county seat. It was the largest county in the world. Frederick included the area that later became the eastern panhandle of West Virginia, with Winchester as its county seat.

On December 13, 1753, Hampshire County was created from Augusta and Frederick counties. Hampshire is the oldest county in the state of West Virginia. Thirty-three years later, in February 1786, Hampshire County was divided into two counties, with the southernmost half forming Hardy County. The Virginia General Assembly chartered Moorefield as the county seat of Hardy County in 1777. The town was located on Conrad Moore's land and named in his honor. The western segment of Hardy County became Grant County on February 14, 1866.

The formation of Hampshire County became effective May 1, 1754. Up until this time all the South Branch, Patterson Creek, New Creek and Capon River valleys had been part of Frederick County.

This area was part of the Northern Neck of Virginia, belonging to Lord Thomas Fairfax. He and the settlers in the remote sections were eager to have a new county created so it would bring the seat of justice closer to the people. Before the creation of Hampshire County, Winchester was the county seat for the entire area. A county government on the South Branch would make it easier to defend the frontier against the Indians who crossed the western mountains and marauded into the country at the beginning of the French and Indian War. It was a simple task to persuade the General Assembly of Virginia to create Hampshire County out of that part of the county of Augusta that lay within the Northern Neck, and from a part of Frederick County.

On November 12, 1762, a petition for a town of fifty acres, which was laid off by Lord Fairfax at Pearsall's Level, was introduced in the General Assembly of Virginia. After three readings of the bill, Governor Francis Fauquier signed it on December 23, 1762, and Romney was established.

Apparently, no separate town government was had by the new town until December 4, 1789, when the General Assembly of Virginia passed an act providing for a board of trustees made up of Isaac Parsons, Isaac Miller, Andrew Woodrow, Stephen Colven, Jonathan Purcell, Nicholas Casey, William McGuire, Purez Drew and James Murphy. (http://www.polsci.wvu.edu/wv/Hampshire/hamhistory.html) Most likely, the Isaac Parsons who was appointed trustee to the town of Romney is the second son of Thomas Parsons Jr. This Isaac Parsons was born November 13, 1766, in Hampshire County and would have been twenty-three years of age. (MacCabe 23, 114)
(Grave marker, Bethel Cemetery, Holly Meadows, West Virginia)

THOMAS PARSONS' ESTATE

The records of Hampshire County indicate that Thomas Parsons Sr. had large valuable tracts of land in present-day Hardy and Grant counties. (MacCabe 18) A Hampshire County recorded deed, dated September 8, 1761, shows that Thomas Parsons Sr. was the executor of the will of Daniel Richardson, and as such conveyed to Henry Vanmeter a tract of land on Mill Creek in present-day Hardy County. (MacCabe 18)

A deed from Phillip Brice dated August 6, 1768, conveyed to Thomas Parsons Sr. 400 acres of land on Cabin Lick Run, in present-day Hampshire County. (MacCabe 18) A deed from Luke Collins dated March 13, 1770, conveyed to Thomas Parsons Sr. Lot Number 16 on the South Branch River. This lot is one-mile southwest of the town of Romney. (MacCabe 18) According to this information and his will that follows, Thomas Parsons Sr. lived prior to 1761, in Hampshire County, present-day Grant County.

WILL OF THOMAS PARSONS SR.

The will of Thomas Parsons Sr. was dated May 27, 1771, and recorded March 10, 1772. He passed away at an undetermined time between those dates. Thomas Parsons Sr. devised to his sons Isaac and Baldwin the land near Romney that he had purchased from Luke Collins. He further directed that Nathaniel Kuxandall, John Foreman and William Foreman divide the land between the two because Baldwin was not yet twenty-one years of age. (MacCabe 18)

Thomas Parsons Sr. then gave one hundred pounds to his daughter Elizabeth, the widow of Dr. Heinsman. Parsons directed the following tracts of land to be sold: 200 acres on Mill Creek, a tract on Michael Sees Run in present-day Hardy and Grant counties, and another tract on Lear Coat Creek in present-day Hampshire County. The proceeds of the sale were to be divided between his sons Thomas, James, Isaac, Baldwin, and his daughters, Prudence and Arness. (MacCabe 19)

Parsons directed his personal property be sold, including the Negroes. Along with the proceeds of the sale, all money, bonds, notes and accounts were to be divided between his children. He then devised to his sons-in-law, William Welton and Robert Cunningham, 290 acres on North Mill Creek, adjoining the upper tract in present-day Pendleton County. The signature to his will indicated that on May 27, 1771, Thomas Parsons Sr. must have been a very old man as it was written in especially large unsteady writing. (MacCabe 19)

Chapter III

THOMAS PARSONS JR.

Thomas Parsons Jr. and Mary (Rennick) Parsons

Mary Ann Rennick (first marriage)
Married: December 15, 1759
Eleven children: William, Isaac, George, James, Hester, Margaret (Parsons) Skidmore, Annis, Catherine (Parsons) Goff, Rebecca (Parsons) Rogers, Hulda and Susannah
(MacCabe 23)

Hannah Thomas Taylor (second marriage)
Married: (Unknown)
One child: a daughter
(MacCabe 23)

Elsie Miles (third marriage)
Married: 1782 (MacCabe 291)
Nine children: Sarah (Parsons) Long, Hannah, Mary (Parsons) Hinkle, Jane (Parsons) Hinkle, Pamelia (Parsons) Welton, Prudence (Parsons) Stump, Elizabeth (Parsons) Brink, Miles and Thomas
(MacCabe 23, 234, 235, 291)

Thomas Parsons Jr. Born November 11, 1730, Moorefield, Virginia
(Genealogical Society of Utah)
Died November 1, 1804, Moorefield, Virginia
(MacCabe 291)

Mary Ann Rennick: Born about 1740, Lancaster County,
Pennsylvania
Died about 1780, Moorefield, Virginia
(Genealogical Society of Utah)

Hannah Thomas Taylor: Born (unknown)
Died (unknown)

Elsie Miles: Born (unknown) Hardy County, Virginia
Died January 19, 1824, Hardy County, Virginia
(MacCabe 291)

Thomas Parsons Jr. is the eldest son of Thomas Parsons Sr. and
Mary Ann (Rennick) Parsons is the daughter of Thomas and Mary
Ann Rennick.

The Parsons plantation was located about seven miles from
Moorefield, Virginia, on the South Branch of the Potomac.

Thomas Parsons Jr. is the maternal great-great-grandfather of
Worley Parsons.

PARSONSES IN HARDY COUNTY

The Parsonses lived in that part of Hampshire County, Virginia, that is present-day Hardy County. In the western third of Hardy County, a small river, known as the Moorefield River, joins the South Branch River. On the flood plain of this river junction lays the town of Moorefield that was established in 1777.

It is obvious that travel was common throughout Hardy County in the late 1700s, as shown by the number of ferries. At that time bridges were few and the settlers, who had cause to cross the large streams, did so by boat. As best we know, in the year 1790 there were eight public ferries listed in Hardy County. (Maxwell and Swisher 280)

There was a public ferry across the South Branch at the homestead of Isaac Parsons, and the legal toll rate was six cents for a man or horse at Parsons' ferry. (Moore 71) A schedule of tolls existed for vehicles of all kinds, including sheep, hogs and cattle. The rate was established by law and the penalty was severe for an overcharge on the part of the ferryman. (Maxwell and Swisher 280)

Men and women of varied backgrounds left their names on the Hardy County scene by 1755. Some left their mark in deed books and wills. In a few short years they had domesticated the wilderness, making plantations and mills the landmarks for roads that linked them to merchants and courthouses. The record of their lives is far more difficult to trace than their surveys and patents. The inventories and last wills of a few of these settlers permit a glimpse of their everyday lives. (MacMaster 30)

In 1751, John Mills owned three horses, a rifle, saddle, bridle, gun barrel and lock, a pair of stockings, a pair of britches, a coat, a shirt, a handkerchief, lead and a powder horn. Robert Fryer, who died in 1753, left horses, rifles, linen shirt and leather britches, a pocket compass and axes. John Scott owned little more than horses, a rifle and a spinning wheel. William Claypool of Hardy County died at the hands of Indians. Francis McBride, Andrew Sadowski, and John McDonald made an inventory of Claypool's possession in March 1758. From it we learn that Claypool raised both flax and grain. He had three horses, five mares and four colts, as well as six heifers, a steer, a cow, and two calves. This was about average. Horses and cattle pastured on the open range of large, unfenced landholdings. He owned no sheep at his death, but he did have "a pair of cards" that might be used to comb fleece as the first stage in spinning wool. The appraisers noted the usual pots and tools, a Bible, a New Testament, an inkhorn, a gun and indigo. (MacMaster 31)

From documents like these that relate to the estates of people who died on the South Branch, a picture slowly emerges of the life and work of the pioneers. Some early settlers apparently lived the hard life associated with the pioneer farm family and many died young. On the other hand, not all pioneers were poor. Some owned Negro men and women. Some had Testaments, books, pewter, bedsteads and bedding, iron pots, cradles and perhaps even a looking glass. But, these were unusual luxuries in the 1750s. For some settlers, wealth was counted exclusively in livestock; but horses and cattle belonged to the poor farmers as well as their more prosperous neighbors.

Auction sales or venues drew large crowds and were normally accompanied by a free flow of spirits. At the event held at Michael Stump's on the South Fork in December 1757, when fear of Indians might have held some back, forty-five people purchased goods at the sale. Their names suggest that they came from various places on the South Branch and the South Fork. Thomas Parsons is listed among those who attended the sale. (MacMaster 33)

ISAAC PARSONS

TUCKER COUNTY'S FIRST SCHOOL

Isaac Parsons (1766-1843) is the second son of Thomas Parsons Jr. and Mary (Rennick) Parsons. His wife was Mary Mace (1771-1851), and they had fourteen children: Mary Ann, Thomas, Drusilla, Jonathan, Rebecca, George M., Catherine, Twins Elizabeth and Jemima, Christina, Twins John H. and William J., Nicholas M. and Nancy Rust. (MacCabe 114) (Grave markers, Bethel Cemetery, Holly Meadows, West Virginia)

Isaac was born in Hardy County, Virginia. After his marriage to Mary Mace, they moved to Randolph County, Virginia, on a plantation at the mouth of Horseshoe Run that he had inherited from his father. He built a two-story log house with stone chimneys that was considered a mansion in that day. (MacCabe 113)

In 1815, Isaac began the first school in Tucker County in an old abandoned building on his farm. It was called the Coburn Run School and was located near the mouth of Coburn Run at Pleasant Vale, five miles from St. George. Coburn Run was a little run emptying into Horseshoe Run from the south. (Fansler 510, 613)

His son Nicholas declared that every pupil was in school by daybreak and remained until dusk, with each one having fifty recitations a day. Nevertheless, it must have been an inadequate education as Nicholas Parsons could not spell his own name and wrote it as "Niclas." (Fansler 614)

Arnold Bonnifield is believed to be the first teacher in Tucker County and taught a few terms at the Coburn Run School. It was not uncommon for pupils in these days to be over twenty-one years of age and the teachers under sixteen years. (Fansler 614)

What was to become Tucker County's first public school, Low Gap was built in 1859. It was located a half-mile northeast of the mouth of Horseshoe Run above the road and about 200 yards south of the triple intersection of the Leadmine-St. George-Parsons roads. All the early schools in Tucker County, including Low Gap, were private until 1863, when the new state of West Virginia's constitution required public education. (Fansler 616)

Nicholas Parsons, his brother George, Rufus Maxwell and David Bonnifield built the Low Gap School. Maxwell donated the lumber, and neighbors supplied the labor. It was the first schoolhouse in Tucker County to have a blackboard. However, the blackboard was fiercely opposed until the teacher, Jennie Blue, demonstrated it at a public exhibition. (Fansler 616)

George Parsons opposed taxation for the purpose of teacher salary. He voted against all school levies; however, he donated generously for the support of schools. But in 1879, Parsons' home was destroyed by fire, and George came with a wagon and dismantled the Low Gap schoolhouse. He hauled it away to rebuild his home. It was logical to George that if the county insisted on levying taxes to build schools, he would confiscate his school. Of course, in taking the school, he also took the shares of the other men who had helped to build it. George Parsons lived to be eighty-five years of age and never married. (Fansler 616, 617)

Isaac Parsons was a founder of the Bethel Church, the first church built in Tucker County. Isaac and his devoted wife, Mary, are interred in the Bethel Cemetery. (MacCabe 113) (Grave marker, Bethel Cemetery, Holly Meadows, West Virginia)

THOMAS PARSONS
AND ROBERT MAXWELL

Fansler says: Robert Maxwell, farmer, preacher, lawyer, and doctor, is credited with building the first home on Horseshoe Run. He built it in 1774 and it is a wonder the Indians didn't kill him as he was living during the entire Dunmore War, within sight of the Seneca Trail. Somehow he escaped although he did return to the South Branch about the time the Dunmore War ended and remained there until 1776 before he returned to Horseshoe Run . . . (He) came from Hardy County with the colony of John Minear. He was under contract with his friend, Thomas Parsons, to claim land and then deed it to him. This he did, obtaining a patent of 700 acres which he deeded to Thomas Parsons and this seems to be the original Parsons title to that land. . . Thomas Parsons' farm on the Cheat adjoined that which he acquired from Maxwell and included that land on Horseshoe Run from the Cheat to the Losh place, comprising several farms . . (Maxwell) died in Randolph County in about 1811. (60-61)

Clearly, Robert Maxwell's farm contained 734 acres. Thomas Parsons bequeathed 470 acres on Maxwell Run to his sons, Miles and Thomas, in his will that was probated in 1804. Sometime previously, he deeded 264 acres of land to his son Isaac. Fansler had a copy of the deed that read: "Thomas Parsons and Wife, deed to Isaac Parsons, 264 acres: Granted by the commonwealth to Thomas Parsons 28th of April 1784, lying and being in the county of Randolph on the Horse Shoe Run including said Thomas Parsons Settlement made thereon in the year 1774, and bounded as follow To wit: Beginning..." It was dated July 10, 1799. (61)

14

WILL OF THOMAS PARSONS JR.

In the name of God, Amen. I, Thomas Parsons, of the County of Hardy and State of West Virginia, being in perfect health and sound memory, thanks be to God for his mercy, calling unto mind the mortality of my body and knowing that it is appointed for all men once to die, do first recommend my soul unto God that gave it, and as far as my body I recommend it to the earth, from whence it came, to be buried in a Christian-like decent manner at the discretion of my executors, nothing doubting but at the General Resurrection I shall receive the same again by the Mighty Power of God and as touching such worldly estate wherewith it has pleased God to bless me with in this life, I give, devise and dispose of the same in the following manner and form:

Imprimis 1st, I give and bequeath unto William Parsons, my first-born son, one plantation lying on Cheat River, which is the whole of his share.

Item 2nd- I give unto Isaac Parsons, my second son, one plantation on the mouth of Horse Shoe Run, which is the whole of his share.

Item 3rd- I give unto George Parsons, my third son, one plantation, adjoining his brother James Parsons' plantation on Cheat River, which is the whole of his share.

Item 4th- I give unto James Parsons, my fourth son, one plantation on Cheat River known by the name of Sims Bottom, lying on both sides of the river, which is the whole of his share.

Item 5th- I give unto my seven eldest daughters, Hester, Margaret, Annas, Catherine, Rebecca, Hulda and Susannah, eleven hundred and sixteen acres to be equally divided amongst them, the land lying on the Middle Fork of the Big Steexe Creek, in Monongalia County.

Item 6th- I give unto Miles Parsons, my fifth son, the full half of my plantation whereon I now live, his part to be taken off of the lower end, likewise one Negro fellow named David, and the full half of a tract of land, 470 acres lying on the head of Maxwell's Run, 235 acres.

Item 7th- I give unto Thomas Parsons, my sixth son, the upper half of my plantation whereon I now live, likewise one Negro fellow named Sampson, and the full half of a tract of land lying on the head of Maxwell's Run containing 470 acres ....235 acres, but in case of the above said Miles Parsons, Thomas Parsons or either of them should die without an heir the above land and Negroes to fall to the other four brothers, but if only the one should die, the land and the Negroes to fall to the survivor of the two.

My houses and lot in the town of Norefield (Moorefield) and the remainder of my Negroes to be sold when my youngest daughter, Elizabeth, shall arrive at the age of sixteen, the houses and lot to be rented until said time and the money arising there from to discharge my youngest daughter's portion as they shall become of age, Sarah, Hannah, Jane, Mary, Pamelia, Prudence and Elizabeth Parsons, which must be learned to read and write.

Item 8th- I give unto my beloved wife, Alsia Parsons, her bedstead and furniture and her third of my plantation I now live on, and her third of all my movables to hold the whole in her possession as long as she remains my widow, the remainder of my movable to be sold to discharge my debts and funeral expenses, my two youngest sons to be taught to read and write and cipher as far as the Golden Rule of Three.

I do make, constitute and appoint my beloved wife, Alsia Parsons, Adam Fisher and my beloved son, William Parsons, my sole executors of this my last will and testament.

In witness whereof, I have hereunto set my hand and seal this twenty-fourth day of September, in the year of our Lord one thousand eight hundred, (1800).

Signed, sealed, published, declared and pronounced by the said Thomas Parsons as his last will and testament in his presence of us, Martin Leonard, Samuel White, Robert Porter, X (his mark).

At a Court held for Hardy County on the 12th day of December, 1804...
Book No. 1, p.292 (MacCabe 21-23)

Chapter IV

WILLIAM PARSONS

William Parsons and Catherine (Stoker) Parsons

Married: April 5, 1785
Nine children: Elizabeth (Parsons) Taggart, Mary (Parsons) Taggart,
Job, Hannah (Parsons) Parsons, Solomon, Nancy (Parsons) Daniels,
Annis (Parsons) Miles, Isaac and Malinda (Parsons) Ball
(MacCabe 27)

William Parsons: Born September 25, 1760, Hampshire County,
Virginia
Died September 10, 1829, Randolph County, Virginia
(MacCabe 27)

Catherine Stoker: Born April 3, 1761, Hampshire County, Virginia
Died (unknown), Randolph County, Virginia
(MacCabe 25, 27)

William Parsons is the maternal great-grandfather of Worley
Parsons.

WILLIAM PARSONS IN RANDOLPH COUNTY, VIRGINIA

W illiam Parsons is the first-born son of Thomas Parsons Jr. and Mary (Rennick) Parsons. He was born in Hampshire County, Virginia, on September 25, 1760. (MacCabe 24)

At one time there were six American Revolution soldiers who made their permanent home in Tucker County: Henry Fansler, David Minear, Salathiel Goff, Samuel Bonnifield, Ambrose Lipscomb and William Parsons. None were born in Tucker County, but five are buried here. (Fansler 640)

On February 6, 1777, at seventeen years of age, William enlisted in the Third Regiment of Light Dragoons, Continental Army, and was commissioned lieutenant on November 1, 1777. He was promoted to captain after the Battle of Eutaw, and served as such for the remainder of the war. William was allotted three hundred acres of land and six hundred dollars in recognition of his service. (MacCabe 24)

Eutawville, South Carolina, about fifty-five miles from Charleston, lies on high ground near the Santee River in a region abounding in swamps, limestone cliffs and pine forests. In colonial days it was a settlement of aristocratic rice planters.

On September 8, 1781, the last battle was fought in the field in the Southern States during the War of American Independence. About 2,300 Americans under General Nathaniel Greene attacked a slightly inferior force under Colonel Alexander Stewart. At first the Americans drove the British before them, but later in the day, the latter took a position in a brick house and behind the palisades. From this position the Americans were unable to drive them. On the night of September 9, however, Colonel Stewart retreated toward

Charleston, abandoning 1,000 stand of arms. The battle has been classed as a tactical victory for the British and a strategic victory for the Americans, terminating a campaign that left General Greene in virtual possession of the Carolinas, the British thereafter confining themselves to Charleston. In killed or wounded, the Americans lost 408 men, including Colonel William Washington who was wounded and captured. The British lost 693 men.

William married Catherine Stoker on April 5, 1785, when he returned from the military. In 1796, he moved his family to Randolph County, Virginia, and settled on his father's land in Holly Meadows. Without delay, he built a log cabin and prepared a comfortable home for his family. Sometime later, William built the first brick home in Tucker County. It was considered a mansion in that day. The house stood until 1947. (Fansler 640)

William was appointed county judge, and those who came under his jurisdiction were usually pleased. It was William's intention to bring the disputing parties together and settle the issue out of court. (MacCabe 23)

With the absence of the Episcopalian denomination in their new home, William and his family united with the Methodist Episcopal Church. He became one of the most prominent members and generously supported the building of the Bethel Church. (MacCabe 24-25)

William is buried in the Bethel Cemetery in Holly Meadows. MacCabe wrote that Catherine lived many years after William had passed on, and the "...negroes cared for her tenderly." She died at the home of her daughter near Beverly, Virginia. The precise date of her death is unknown. (25) (Grave marker, Bethel Cemetery, Holly Meadows, West Virginia)

WILL OF WILLIAM PARSONS

In the year of our Lord one thousand eight hundred and twenty-eight, January 11th, William Parsons of Randolph County, and State of Virginia, in the presence of Almighty God and in my proper senses, do hereby make my last will and testament, after bequeathing my body to the dust and my soul to God that gave it, I bequeath my property in the following manner, namely: to Job Parsons, my eldest son, I bequeath this tract of land he now lives on; to Solomon, my second son, I bequeath my home place, that is the tract of land I now live on, except one-third of said place which I bequeath to Catherine Parsons, my wife, so long as she lives, to be surveyed off the lower end so as to embrace the house.

To my daughters Elizabeth Taggart, Mary Taggart, Hannah Parsons, Nancy Daniels, Anis Milly and Malinda Parsons I bequeath one thousand dollars each with what I have paid and I may pay against my death to each, to be taken out of said sums, and the balance to be paid after my death. To my three eldest daughters above named I also bequeath a bed and reasonable clothing for said beds apiece, the rest of the household estate to be divided equally amongst the six daughters above named, except my desk I bequeath to Malinda at the appraisement as a part of her thousand, said bequeath not to take place until after the death of my wife. As to the rest of my movable property, I bequeath it in the following manner to be appraised by three disinterested appraisers to be given to my six daughters, (except the wagon Solomon is to have at the appraisement if he desires it) above named as part of the thousand dollars I have bequeathed them; provided, nevertheless, if my daughters refuse to take the said property at the appraisement, then the property shall be put up for sale and any of my children may bid it off, and the property of said sale may be applied to paying said daughters their bequeath; provided, nevertheless, that said moveable property shall amount to more than the thousand dollars bequeathed to each of my six daughters, the said remaining property shall be divided equally amongst said six daughters above named.

N.B. I reserve one horse and three cows out of my movable property for Catherine my wife during her lifetime, and then to be disposed of at her death as above directed.

I further direct my administrators to prepare said property and appoint the time for division as soon as convenient.

6th - I bequeath the Island place or tract of land lying a little below my home place to Solomon Parsons, my second son. I also bequeath him a small tract of land against his place on the west side of Shavers Fork, or on the lower end of the place he now lives on.

7th - I further direct that Job Parsons and Solomon Parsons, my sons be appointed as administrators.

8th - I further bequeath my blacks, Titus to live with Catherine my wife and Solomon my son as long as he lives, and that he may be supported, as he is old. Buck, a Negro man, and Emily, a Negro woman, to live and labor for Catherine Parsons my wife as long as she lives, and at her death if Job and Solomon Parsons, my administrators, think they have not by their labor paid for what I gave for them they are to hire them out until they have paid for what I gave for them. If said Buck and Emily should have children they are to go free with them, and the profits of said hire to be equally divided and paid over to my six daughters above named, over and above the thousand dollars I bequeathed to each of them, and if after said Buck and Emily have paid for their price I paid, they and their children are to go free. I further direct that Solomon, my son, keep them and pay the hire if they have to be hired, and if he does not want to do so to hire them in the family if possible.

N.B. Nevertheless, if there should be on hand at my decease a stock of drove cattle, they are to be fatted and sold to the best advantage by the executors. I further bequeath that Solomon and Job shall have, or my administrators, one year from the time of entering as administrators to commence the payment bequeathed to my daughters, they shall then pay $500.00 per year until all be paid. In witness whereof, I have set my hand and seal this 17th day of January 1828.
William Parsons, (Seal)
Isaac Reynolds, Idonigah Ward, William R. Parsons, Witnesses.
(MacCabe 25-27)

TUCKER COUNTY CENSUS 1860

Thomas B. Rummell, a twenty-one year old attorney from Beverly, Virginia, took the first census of Tucker County in 1860. This was ten years before the first census of West Virginia, as Tucker County is seven years older than the state of West Virginia. (Fansler 95)

At that time Tucker County had three magisterial districts: Hannahsville, St. George and Black Fork. There were seven post offices: Hannahsville, Limestone, St. George, Horseshoe Run, Holly Meadows, Black Fork and Dry Fork. Rummell established that there were 245 families living in Tucker County. The census did not include slaves, although there were 16 slaves in the county at that time who were owned by the Goff and Parsons families. The census included free Negroes. (Fansler 95)

Two Negro families were residing in Tucker County in 1860. One family carried the name Crofton (or Crosten), and the other family was named Parsons. One should consider that during the period of slavery (1619-1865), a Negro was a piece of tangible property who was bought, bred, worked and sold, with only one name. When a slave became too old or sick to work, they were occasionally set free. Infrequently, a slave was freed in appreciation of faithful service. This was executed by their masters through writs, wills or bills of sale. In the free world surnames were required in regular transactions. They had no surnames, only a given name like Samuel, Buck or George. Suddenly, they found themselves in a situation where they were required to have a proper name. It was quite natural for the Negro to adopt the surname of the former owner. (Fansler 96)

PARSONSES IN TUCKER COUNTY

Following is a record of sixteen Parsons families who resided in Tucker County when the 1860 Census was taken. They were registered under the district and post office where they lived.

Hannahsville District – Hannahsville Post Office

House Number 9

Family	Age	Birthplace
Parsons, George (Negro)	25	Virginia
Parsons, Mary (Negro)	23	Virginia
Parsons, Franklin (Negro)	5	Virginia
Parsons, Lindsey (Negro)	3	Virginia
Parsons, Sarah E. (Negro)	1	Virginia

(Fansler 101)

Above are listed the descendents of what were believed to be the freed slaves of William Parsons. The number that William Parsons set free is unknown.   (Fansler 96)

Slavery was not economical in western Virginia, as most people engaged in farming and livestock. The larger farms of tobacco and other cash crops used slaves. African-American populations in West Virginia in 1860 totaled 21,144; of those 2,773 were free and 18,371 were enslaved. Tucker County showed 36 African Americans, 16 free and 20 enslaved. Neighboring Randolph County showed a total of 197, 14 free and 183 enslaved.
(http://www.wvculture.org/history/blackpop.html)

Saint George District – Horseshoe Run Post Office

House Number 94

Family	Age	Birthplace
Parsons, Nicholas M.	48	Virginia
Parsons, George H.	50	Virginia
Parsons, Rebecca	60	Virginia
Parsons, Elizabeth	55	Virginia
Parsons, Nancy	35	Virginia
Parsons, Hampton	30	Virginia
Parsons, Adaline	26	Virginia
Parsons, Edgar H.	22	Virginia
Parsons, Charles	17	Virginia
Colyer, Perry	16	Virginia

(Fansler 109)

Nicholas M. Parsons (1812-1897), George H. Parsons (1808-1887), Rebecca Parsons (1797-1880), Elizabeth Parsons (1805-1881) and Nancy Parsons (1815-1883) were unmarried and living at home in 1860. They are the children of Isaac and Mary (Mace) Parsons and grandchildren of Thomas Parsons Jr. (MacCabe 114) (Grave markers, Bethel Cemetery, Holly Meadows, West Virginia)

Nicholas was born on his father's plantation at the mouth of Horseshoe Run. Sometime later, he built a grand two-story home near the old family home. Parsons owned over sixteen hundred acres of land but lost a significant amount of property during the Civil War, as a southern sympathizer. At seventy years of age, he married twenty-one year old Regania Teter on May 11, 1882. (MacCabe 126)

In the past oak rails were rafted down the Cheat in large quantities. Nicholas once cut a lot of rail timber, hauled it to the bank of the river and placed it on skids inclined toward the river. When all was ready, the prop that held the first log was knocked out, and all the logs skidded into the water and instantly sank to the bottom. (Maxwell 147)

Saint George District – Saint George Post Office

House Number 101

Family	Age	Birthplace
Parsons, Solomon	66	Virginia
Parsons, Hannah	69	Virginia
Tyre, Nancy	19	Virginia
Stuckey, Joseph	16	Virginia
Stuckey, Anamelia	13	Virginia

(Fansler 110)

Dr. Solomon Parsons is the son of Captain James Parsons and Rebecca (Simps) Parsons. He married Hannah, a granddaughter of Thomas Parsons Jr. on August 20, 1810. Nancy Tyre, Joseph and Anamelia Stuckey were most likely paid servants, as Parsons was greatly opposed to slavery. Dr. Solomon Parsons' family will be addressed later in this book. (MacCabe 241)

Saint George District – Saint George Post Office

House Number 162

Family	Age	Birthplace
Parsons, James W.	49	Virginia
Parsons, Ann E.	48	Virginia
Parsons, Sansome E.	21	Virginia
Parsons, Hannah A.	19	Virginia
Parsons, Helen L.	17	Virginia
Parsons, Ann	14	Virginia
Parsons, Solomon J.	10	Virginia
Parsons, Dianna E.	7	Virginia

(Fansler 116)

James William Parsons is the son of Dr. Solomon Parsons and Hannah. His first marriage was to Catherine A. Neville on May 29, 1832. They had nine children; six are listed above. His second marriage was to Ann Eliza Prentis. James W. Parsons' family will be discussed later in this work. (MacCabe 242)

Saint George District – Saint George Post Office

House Number 163

Family	Age	Birthplace
Parsons, William R.	63	Virginia
Parsons, Nelson	24	Virginia
Parsons, Rebecca	23	Virginia
Parsons, Rachel	22	Virginia
Parsons, John	20	Virginia
Parsons, Joseph	19	Virginia
Parsons, Eldridge	17	Virginia
Parsons, David B.	14	Virginia
Parsons, Mary J.	12	Virginia

(Fansler 116)

William Rust Parsons (1798-1881) is the first son of James and Nancy (Rust) Parsons and grandson of Thomas Parsons Jr. His first marriage was to Catherine Ward (1801-1833) on June 6, 1824, and they had four children. William's second wife was Mary Crouch, and the children from that union are listed above. (MacCabe 144-145)

William was born in Hardy County, Virginia. At two years of age, his parents migrated to Randolph County, Virginia. His formative years were spent on the home plantation that embraced the banks of the Cheat River at Simm's Bottom. (MacCabe 143)

When the Virginia General Assembly passed the act forming Tucker County in 1856, William Rust Parsons was appointed commissioner, along with four others, to organize the new county. (Fansler 219) On April 3, 1862, without opposition, Parsons was elected justice of Black Fork district. (Fansler 224) However, in the October 1864 election, Daniel C. Adams was elected assessor with three less votes than William Rust Parsons. Adams was a Union man, while Parsons was a Confederate and slave owner. (Fansler 230)

William owned a large tract of land in Sugarlands that was covered with black maple sugar trees and other valuable timber. Abe Bonnifield described the property as follows: "About fifteen hundred acres of the land was purchased by William R. Parsons, and the sugar trees have fallen beneath the axes of his slaves. But, thank kind nature, it is usually the case, when one beautiful object disappears, another takes it place. Although the sugar trees are gone, the eye of the spectator is now greeted with green pastures and charming meadows, while the ear is saluted with the tinkling of bells and the lowing of cattle, and this delightful Sugar Lands promises fair soon to be the riches grazing plantation in Tucker County." (Maxwell 168)

Parsons lived on a farm in the Horseshoe Bend. The land had been purchased by his father from Isaac Parsons, son of Captain James Parsons. (MacCabe 139)

When the emancipation of slaves was declared, he called his slaves together and offered them the same homes and treatment they had always enjoyed. However, they would have nothing to do with it and left promptly. (Fansler 230)

As a southern sympathizer, William suffered heavily during the Civil War. His assessment by Captain Kellogg was $800 to make good the losses incurred by the Union men. The order warned: "If you fail to pay in three days, your property will all be confiscated, your house burned and yourself shot." By order of Brigadier General Millroy, Captain Kellogg, Commanding 123rd Ohio. But Parsons informed the officer that it was impossible for him to pay the amount; he "could only die but once". (MacCabe 143)

Nelson Parsons (1836-1862) is the first son of William R. Parsons. He enlisted in the Confederate army in May 1861 and served with Lieutenant Robert McChesney at the first skirmish fought in West Virginia when Lieutenant McChesney was killed. (MacCabe 149)

Saint George District – Saint George Post Office

House Number 165

Family	Age	Birthplace
Parsons, Jesse	35	Virginia
Parsons, Catherine	30	Virginia
Parsons, William	10	Virginia
Parsons, Mary S.	3	Virginia

(Fansler 116)

Jesse Parsons (1825-1896) is the first son of William R. Parsons and Catherine (Ward) Parsons and great-grandson of Thomas Parsons Jr. (MacCabe 144) He married Catherine Parsons (1829-1895) on September 30, 1847, and they had nine children. Catherine is the sister of Ward Parsons for whom the town of Parsons was named. (MacCabe 146)

Tucker County's first election was held on May 22, 1856. At that time, there were no nominations, primaries, parties or ballots. A candidate solicited votes for himself, and the ballots were all write-ins. Jesse Parsons, a fervent and loyal Democrat, defeated William Corrick, 92 to 65, to be elected the first sheriff of Tucker County. He served two consecutive terms 1856-1858 and 1858 to 1860. (Fansler 219, 220, 236)

Jesse was taken prisoner during the Civil War. On August 13, 1861, a Federal force of about one hundred men led by George R. Latham of Company B 2nd (West) Virginia Infantry, was sent from Grafton to Tucker County. They came for the purpose of obtaining mounts for the reorganization of a cavalry regiment. During the raid, they seized fifteen civilian prisoners, muskets, horses and ammunition. Many farmers in Holly Meadows suffered the loss of their finest horses, and several of them were taken prisoner and held for weeks. Jesse was among those detained. (Fansler 191)

Saint George District – Saint George Post Office

House Number 166

Family	Age	Birthplace
Parsons, Andrew B.	43	Virginia
Parsons, Phoebe A.	39	New York
Parsons, Jesse	15	Virginia
Parsons, Jane	13	Virginia
Parsons, Abraham	11	Virginia
Parsons, James W.	9	Virginia
Parsons, Sarah E.	7	Virginia
Parsons, Nancy C.	5	Virginia
Parsons, Columbia	3	Virginia
Parsons, Laura	1	Virginia

(Fansler 116-117)

Andrew B. Parsons (1816-1894) is the eighth son of James and Nancy (Rust) Parsons and grandson of Thomas Parsons Jr. His first marriage was to Phoebe Ann Howe (1821-1881) on September 5, 1844. His second wife was Annie W. Ware. (MacCabe 222)

Andrew was born on the plantation on the banks of the Cheat River at Simm's Bottom. Early on, he assumed the responsibility of his father's plantation and tenderly cared for his parents until they passed on. (MacCabe 221)

In 1858, James Parsons bequeathed to Andrew a tract of sixty-eight acres of land on Simm's Bottom, one-half of a tract of 400 acres on the west side of Cheat River on Branon's Run, and one-half of a tract of 140 acres of land on Otter Fork. Andrew inherited the homeplace. In October 1876, he sold the land and migrated to California. This land had been in the Parsons family for many generations. "Twenty children of two generations were reared in the log house, built in 1800... Forty-five children were born on this plantation, and thirty-five little pickaninnies were born in the cabins." (MacCabe 139, 142, 221)

Saint George District – Saint George Post Office

House Number 167

Family	Age	Birthplace
Parsons, Ward	33	Virginia
Parsons, Sarah A.	30	Virginia
Parsons, Lloyd	11	Virginia
Parsons, Catherine B.	4	Virginia
Parsons, Mary C.	2	Virginia
Parsons, Elizabeth	3mos	Virginia

(Fansler 117)

Ward Parsons (1827-1898) is the third son of Solomon Parsons and Mary (Ward) Parsons and great-grandson of Thomas Parsons Jr. Ward married a cousin, Sarah Anne Parsons (1828-1910), who is a daughter of William Rust and Catherine (Ward) Parsons, on October 14, 1847. They were the parents of eight children.   (MacCabe 101)

Parsons, the third settler in the town of Parsons, built a log house near the intersection of Fifth and Main streets, about the time he was married. Fansler says that his grandmother, Anna Ward, heard the guns at Corricks Ford from the dwelling, which accidentally burned in 1896.   (Fansler 378- 379)

Ward Parsons was a radical Confederate who voted for secession in the spring of 1861. He owned over 1,000 acres of land and many fine horses. Ward was continually harassed during the Civil War. During one raid, Lanham's men surrounded his property and began shooting. Parsons rushed from the house and ran for the Shavers Fork River, through an assault of minie-balls. He leaped the river's embankment and fell as though he were dead. By the time the Yankees searched for him, he had escaped. But he lost horses, cattle and much of his property during the course of the war. (Fansler 192)

The city of Parsons was named for Ward Parsons. According to Fansler, "Before the town was incorporated it had a post office named 'Job,' which was located in the Cheat River Hotel, where the courthouse now stands, and Sansome E. Parsons was the postmaster. It was named for aged Job Parsons Sr., the father-in-law of Abraham Parsons. Job Ward Parsons I, a son of Abraham Parsons, had purchased a stock farm on Dry Fork River, 5 ½ miles above Harman, and had a fourth class post office in his store there which he named 'Parsons,' and of which he was postmaster. Ballyhoo artist Ward Parsons approached stock farmer Job Ward Parsons for a swap of post office names, and after some haggling the deal was made and approved by the Post Office Department . . . Lemuel Ward Parsons, son of Ward Parsons said the decision was made by cutting high card. Ward cut first and turned the trey of hearts; he started to walk away in disgust when Job turned the deuce of spades." (382)

Ward and Sarah Parsons were devoted to the community and church; she taught Sunday school for several years. The First United Methodist Church of Parsons was originally named the Methodist Episcopal Church, North. The church was built in 1892 on land purchased from Ward and Sarah Parsons for the sum of fifty dollars. (History of the First United Methodist Church 1892-1992, Tucker County Deed Book 12, pp. 199-200)

Ward Parsons passed away February 24, 1898, on his seventy-first birthday. He and his devoted wife, Sarah Ann, are interred in the Bethel Cemetery. (Grave marker, Bethel Cemetery, Holly Meadows, West Virginia)

Black Fork District – Holly Meadows Post Office

House Number 172

Family	Age	Birthplace
Parsons, Washington	26	Virginia
Parsons, Martha M.	25	Virginia
Parsons, Nancy S.	3	Virginia
Parsons, Emaline	1	Virginia
Parsons, Wellington	3 months	Virginia
Peppers, Mary	12	Virginia
Long, Georgiana	7	Virginia

(Fansler 117)

Washington Parsons (1834-1912) is the first son of Abraham and Emily Parsons and great-grandson of Thomas Parsons Jr. He married Martha (Bond) Long (1834-1911) on November 13, 1856. Martha is a daughter of William and Martha Bond. (MacCabe 185-186)

Washington Parsons was ten years of age when his parents moved to Parsons. After his marriage to Martha, they moved to the farm where the Battle of Corrick's Ford was fought on July 13, 1861. Their home was converted into a hospital and their household goods carried away. Washington, with his wife and four children, fled over the mountains as shots whistled over their heads. (MacCabe 185)

On his return home, Washington Parsons found a big Negro walking around wearing his wedding suit. But he dared not approach him, as it would have been considered disloyal. Martha had searched the camps near Beverly for her stolen horse, and on her return home, noticed a few straggling soldiers making off with her turkey hen. Martha jumped the fence and captured the bird. "Another battle won by a rebel!" Washington Parsons and his family migrated to California in 1872 and settled in Monterey County. (MacCabe 185)

Black Fork District – Holly Meadows Post Office

House Number 185

Family	Age	Birthplace
Parsons, James R.	46	Virginia
Parsons, Mahala	46	Virginia
Parsons, Cornelius	21	Virginia
Parsons, Susannah	19	Virginia
Parsons, Marcella	18	Virginia
Parsons, Nancy	17	Virginia
Parsons, Luther	15	Virginia
Parsons, Joshua	14	Virginia
Parsons, Robert	12	Virginia
Parsons, Thomas	11	Virginia
Parsons, Emily	8	Virginia
Parsons, Harriet	6	Virginia

(Fansler 118-119)

James Rust Parsons (1814-1887) is the seventh son of James and Nancy (Rust) Parsons and the grandson of Thomas Parsons Jr. He married Mahala Mason in 1838, and they had ten children (MacCabe 215)

Known as "Tanner Jim," he operated a profitable tannery that had been erected by his father on the plantation. He manufactured leather for footwear and harness and had a thriving business until the entire establishment was destroyed by fire. He then purchased a 450-acre farm on Shavers Fork and engaged in farming. (MacCabe 214)

After General Garnett's death and the defense at Corricks Ford collapsed, July 1861, two companies of the 1st Georgia Regiment were cut off from the main army. Parsons found them on McGowan Mountain, south of present-day Hendricks, wandering up the mountainside in the pouring rain. They were starved and reduced to eating roots and bark. Parsons furnished them with food and guided them over the mountains to Monterey, Virginia. For this, he fell into disfavor. He left Tucker County and returned following the war. (Fansler 165)

Black Fork District – Holly Meadows Post Office

House Number 191

Family	Age	Birthplace
Parsons, Abraham	50	Virginia
Parsons, Emily	42	Virginia
Parsons, Harriet	20	Virginia
Parsons, Elizabeth	18	Virginia
Parsons, Mahala	16	Virginia
Parsons, James	15	Virginia
Parsons, Jacob	13	Virginia
Parsons, Virginia	11	Virginia
Parsons, Phoebe	3	Virginia

(Fansler 119)

Abraham Parsons (1809-1884) is the sixth son of James and Nancy (Rust) Parsons and grandson of Thomas Parsons Jr. He married Emily (Parsons) Parsons (1817-1898) on February 12, 1834, when she was sixteen years of age, and they became the parents of eleven children. Emily is the second daughter of Job Parsons Sr. and Jemima (Ward) Parsons.   (MacCabe 43, 183-184)

In April 1884, Abraham moved from the homestead in Randolph County to a 125-acre farm in Parsons between Shavers Fork and Black Fork Rivers. A record in the Randolph County Clerk's office reads that he purchased the farm from his father-in-law, Job Parsons Sr. for $1,500. Abraham erected a log home and combined grist-sawmill, along Billings Avenue, that was water-powered by a natural sluice. The mill was destroyed in 1857 by flood and a new mill was built two years later. It weathered the unexpected changes that occurred during the Civil War and was relocated at the corner of Billings Avenue and Railroad Street. It remained in operation under new owners until 1920. An old buhr stone can still be seen as you pass through Parsons today. Abraham Parsons was the second settler to Parsons.   (MacCabe 183) (Fansler 377-378)

Abraham Parsons was a radical Confederate that voted for secession in 1861. Union neighbors reported him as disloyal to the

Restored Government, and soon troops came to seize his property. They wrecked his mill and marched him the thirty miles to a jail in Beverly. He gave a lad a quarter to carry a note to his cousin Mary E. Buckley who lived nearby. She immediately brought warm food and blankets. After three weeks in the Beverly jail, Abraham was moved to Camp Chase, Ohio, the Yankee "Andersonville." (MacCabe 183)

Camp Chase was a Civil War camp established in May 1861 and built on the western outskirts of Columbus, Ohio. The camp received its first large influx of captured Confederates from western campaigns, including enlisted men, officers, and a few of the latter's black servants. In 1862, nearly 1,100 enlisted men were held there. The men were divided into messes of eighteen men that were housed in small buildings, twenty feet by fourteen feet, scattered across the prison grounds in clusters of six, with narrow alleys separating the clusters. The buildings leaked, ventilation was poor, and water gathered beneath the floorboards of the buildings when it rained. Prisoners even cooked their meals in the small buildings. As the war wore on, conditions deteriorated. Original facilities for 3,500-4,000 men were jammed with close to 7,000, and as many as 10,000 prisoners were confined there by the time the Confederates surrendered. In 1863, Camp Chase Confederate Cemetery was established and over 2,000 Confederate soldiers' graves can be found there. (http://WWW.censusdiggins.com/prison_campchase.html)

Abraham's son secured his release by petitioning the Governor. When he finally returned home, his health was impaired by starvation to the degree that his wife was unable to recognize him. Even then, he was harassed almost continually by Unionists until the end of the war. (MacCabe 183-184)

Abraham sold his property to Abraham Currence of Randolph County and with eighteen family members moved to Gonzales, California, in November 1872. There he died on August 19, 1884, and is buried in the Gonzales Cemetery. (Fansler 378)

VIRGINIA PARSONS MACCABE

Virginia Parsons (1849-1935) is the daughter of Abraham and Emily (Parsons) Parsons. Virginia married William Lohman Parsons (1838-unknown) on June 14, 1870, and they had two children. William is the son of David Miles Parsons (1795-1846) and Jemima (Harness) Parsons of Hardy County (1800-unknown), and grandson of Thomas Parsons Jr. He fought at the battles of Cedar Rapids and Gettysburg. Virginia's second marriage was to Duncan MacCabe (1849-1905) on March 10, 1877, and they had two children. Virginia (Parsons) MacCabe is the author of the *Parsons Family History and Record* that was published in 1913.
(MacCabe 198, 229, 231) (http://www.rootsweb.com/~wvtucker/mgs.htm)

JOB WARD PARSONS

Job Ward Parsons (1838 – unknown) is the third son of Abraham and Emily Parsons. He was born on the James Parsons plantation in Randolph County, Virginia. Job was employed in the wholesale and retail paper store of Edward Towers in Washington, D.C. from March to October of 1859, returning home via Harper's Ferry on the morning of John Brown's capture. (MacCabe 190)

November 1862, Job enlisted in Company A Eighteenth Virginia Cavalry with Captain William H. Taylor in command. Job was appointed second sergeant and detailed by General John D. Imboden as his principal scout. Company A was considered the best in the regiment and fought at Gettysburg; Williamsport, Maryland; New Hope or Piedmont, Virginia; Lynchburg; Winchester; Fisher's Hill; Cedar Creek and New Market. Captain Taylor, who hailed from Randolph County, was killed in the battle of Winchester. The men of Company A petitioned the general requesting that Job Parsons be appointed the commanding officer over three lieutenants. General Imboden honored the request. (MacCabe 191)

In February 1865, they were ordered to report to Lynchburg. When they got within four miles of Lexington, they learned that Lee had surrendered. This was a great disappointment for those that had fought so hard for "the cause." (MacCabe 191)

Job W. Parsons married Mary Elizabeth Smith (1845-1870) on January 1, 1867, and they had two children. His second wife was Mary Jane Ewin (1840-unknown). She is the daughter of William D. Ewin Sr. and Martha Ann (Dennis) Ewin. They were married on June 11, 1872 and had five children: Stella Maud, William Ewin, Job Walter, Jr., Frances Ann, Dickson Ward and Angelica Ewin. (http://www.ewin.org/Family%20Tree.html) (MacCabe 192)

In 1898, Job went to California for a family reunion. In March 1899, Job and his brother James sailed from San Francisco to Valdez, Alaska, in search of gold. They journeyed across Alaska's unexplored territory. From Copper River they traveled by sleds to Dawson and Nome. Later that spring, he returned to California, but in March 1901, he sailed once again. On this voyage, he was accompanied by his sister and nephew. They returned to California in September, and Job went home to Kingwood, West Virginia, where he spent his final days. (MacCabe 191, 197)

CIVIL WAR EXPERIENCES

An Address by Job W. Parsons
Parsons Family Reunion 1908

"Ladies, I was a Confederate soldier from choice. My home was in the main lines during the entire war. I remained at my home for a little over a year after the war began. After deliberate consideration, I decided that Old Virginia called me, and I went to her aid with all my heart. I had from 100 to 120 men in my company, all of the same material. Nine out of ten of them had their homes in the main lines and could have gone home any time, and stayed out the war.

I was 2nd sergeant most of the war, joined the Company after it was organized. General J. D. Imboden detailed me as his principal scout. My duty was to find out the whereabouts of the enemy, and his numbers. In consequence, I have traveled over and know every road and path from Harpers Ferry to the valley to Lonsacks Depot, south to Lynchburg, Roanoke, and Clifton Forge. Company A was considered the best one in the regiment, and when ever any work was to be done that required courage and men, the General always called on Company A, and they never disappointed him.

I was with them in every battle they were in, which included the following: The Battle of Gettysburg; Williamsport, Maryland, the hottest fight I was in during the war, to defend our wagon trains; Battle of New Hope on Piedmont, Augusta Col, Val, (General W. E. Jones was killed here); Lynchburg, then to Washington with General Early; Battle 19 of September with General Gordon, and many other smaller battles.

When General Lee fell back from Gettysburg, after we had stayed at Williamsport, Maryland, five or six days, General Imboden sent for me one evening and told me that General Lee had been informed that General Mead was moving and concentrating his army on Lee's right, and after it got dark he wanted me to take any number of men I wished and go as near the enemy lines or inside of them and remain all night, and come in the morning and report what I had learned. I took three men and traveled all night in a strange country to me, and it was so dark you couldn't see your hand before your nose. I was so close to a picket or two I could hear his horse breathe. I kept my bearings by the roaring of the water pouring over a dam in the Potomac River. Mr. Mead was not moving. We were at Williamsport eight days, and Mr. Mead did not move till the Potomac got low enough for us to ford it on our horses, and when we crossed to Virginia he got very anxious to find us from the other side of the river.

Captain Wm. H. Taylor of Company A was killed in the battle of Winchester. I was by his side when he was shot and fell off his white horse at once. He was one of Randolph County's bravest and noblest sons. He and I were riding side by side in the Battle of Kenstown when a shell from a cannon went between us, burst just as it passed us so close to us that the powder blackened our faces, but the pieces went forward, not back, and we were only stunned by the explosion.

After that the men of Company A, unbeknown to me, got up a petition to the General to make me Captain of the Company, over three lieutenants, and every man in the Company but one signed it. So I was made their commanding officer according to their will. And the next morning as I walked through the camp men, who never noticed me before, officers and all, took off their caps. "How are you Captain?" I was no better man then than I was the day before and it displeased me to see men so foolish over a man's position.

I wish to mention an incident that occurred at the Battle of New Market. General J. C. Breckinridge against General Segal. Just before the battle, we were drawn up in line of battle, the 62nd infantry 950 strong, 18th Virginia Cavalry, and the 23rd Cavalry, both full regiments. Father Brooks, our brigade chaplain, came in front of our line while the bullets were passing and took off his hat and bowed himself on the ground and a more fervent prayer I never heard, praying that the good Lord would confuse, confound, and put our enemies to flight, and that we might scatter them to the four winds of the earth. We had 4,000 and they had 18,000; and we drove them in the open valley for three miles, and scattered them as the old man had prayed; and if they had not burned the bridge at Mt. Jackson behind them, we would have destroyed their whole army.

Just after Father Brooks made his famous prayer, General John C. Breckenridge (and I think he was the finest looking man I ever saw) told

General Imboden we would have to attack then. It was 11:00 a.m. and we could not wait any longer for them to attack us. This is where the Virginia Cadets immortalized themselves. I saw them go into that battle eight abreast with a fine, blue silk flag floating over them, a march into the jaws of death like they did. In the hottest of the battle, they charged a battery of six guns and captured them all while the shot and canister poured through their ranks until they climbed over the guns then and drove the guns away.

In February 1865 I was in Highland County, Virginia, resting, and feeding up our horses – only had my Company. I was ordered to report at Lynchburg for orders, when I got with the company within four miles of Lexington, Virginia. I think it was the 11th day of April 1865. I met an infantryman in the road and he says General Lee had surrendered. I said, "That's not so, Sir!" He put his hand in his vest pocket and drew his printed parole bearing date 10th April Appomattox, Virginia. My heart sank within me. I had never had anything till then that made me feel so bad, and the final end had been defeat. I could hardly realize it could be so. I had pictured in my mind that General Lee would concentrate all his forces and make one grand fight when he was cornered.

I always thought and think today that if Stonewall Jackson had lived and been at Gettysburg, we would have won that fight, which would have changed the whole course of the war. . ."
(Courtesy of Marvin E. Parsons)

Black Fork District – Holly Meadows Post Office

House Number 194

Family	Age	Birthplace
Parsons, Thomas Slack	42	Virginia
Parsons, Elizabeth	30	Virginia
Parsons, Signora	7	Virginia
Parsons, John G. C.	5	Virginia
Parsons, Magarga	2	Virginia

(Fansler 120)

Thomas Slack Parsons (1818-1873) is the youngest son of James and Nancy (Rust) Parsons and grandson of Thomas Parsons Jr. He married Elizabeth Currence (1829-1903) in 1852 and they had nine children. Thomas Slack was the last child of James and Nancy Parsons to be born on his plantation gracing the banks of Cheat River at Simm's Bottom. (MacCabe 227)

MacCabe tells us that: "Many grand functions were given in his (James Parsons) quaint old home in his day; nine sons were given an 'Infare' as they termed it in those days, when they brought home their brides. When the wedding party was within a mile of the groom's home it was the custom for two men to run a race for the bottle. When he brought his bride home his brother Abraham entered the race for the bottle with a man of Tagarts (Tygart) Valley. They rushed over hill and dale thorough the Cheat river, all of the guests and 'darkies' were out to witness this exciting race. Their enthusiasm was at high pitch when Parsons won and triumphantly carried the bottle decorated with a white ribbon, back to the party and presented it to the bride; it was passed to all the party and they drank to the health of the newly wedded pair." (227) (Grave markers, Bethel Cemetery, Holly Meadows, West Virginia) (An Infare is a housewarming, especially one for a bride)

Black Fork District – Holly Meadows Post Office

House Number 195

Family	Age	Birthplace
Parsons, Jacob W.	41	Virginia
Parsons, Jemima W.	30	Virginia
Parsons, Mary M.	13	Virginia
Parsons, Lavernia A.	11	Virginia
Parsons, Manerva C.	8	Virginia
Parsons, Caroline E.	7	Virginia
Parsons, Perry W.	5	Virginia
Parsons, Truman C.	3	Virginia

(Fansler 120)

Jacob Ward Parsons (1819-1896) is the first son of Job Parsons Sr. and Jemima (Ward) Parsons and great-grandson of Thomas Parsons Jr. He was married on December 21, 1843, to Jemima (Parsons) Parsons (1824-1910), and they had eleven children. Jemima is the second daughter of Solomon and Mary (Ward) Parsons, and the great-granddaughter of Thomas Parsons Jr. (MacCabe 46)

After Jacob was married, he purchased some fertile property in the wilderness, built a log home, and started his own grazing farm, which was well stocked with sheep and cattle. His farm brought him immense contentment. But, when the children reached the age to be educated, he wasted no time in moving to Cheat River near the schools. (MacCabe 46)

Parsons held public offices on the Republicans ticket for the following terms: Commissioner (1860-1863) and sheriff (1863-1867). But, Jacob wanted more land. In October 1867, he sold all his Tucker County holdings, moved to Grant County, and purchased large acreage near the home of his 1700 ancestors. His last days were spent in Davis, West Virginia, with his daughter. (MacCabe 46) (Fansler 242-243, 236) (Grave markers, Bethel Cemetery, Holly Meadows, West Virginia)

Black Fork District – Holly Meadows Post Office

House Number 199

Family	Age	Birthplace
Parsons, Job Jr.	40	Virginia
Parsons, Martha	15	Virginia
Parsons, Solomon	9	Virginia

(Fansler 120)

Job Parsons Jr. (1820-1904) is the second son of Solomon and Mary (Ward) Parsons and great-grandson of Thomas Parsons Jr. His first marriage was to Jemima Ward (unknown-1853) on September 2, 1840. They had three children; two are listed above. His second wife was Eunice Jane Long (1841-1912). They married on July 21, 1870, and had seven children. (MacCabe 93-94) (Fansler 374)

Job was born on his father's plantation on Cheat River in Randolph County, Virginia. Solomon, had been in poor health for several years, and passed away when Job was a mere thirteen years of age. With the help of his older brother, William, and the old Negro, he managed the farm well. At that time, there were four children at home: Elizabeth, eleven; Jemima, nine, Ward (for whom the town of Parsons was named), six and Catherine (that married the first sheriff of Parsons), four. Mary Caroline was born five months after Solomon died. (MacCabe 84)

Job Parsons Jr. was a firm Democrat who served as Commissioner of Tucker County for the terms of 1866-1871. Even though his sympathies were with the south during the Civil War, he was not harmed. Job spent his last days on his farm in Holly Meadows. (MacCabe 93) (Fansler 243)

Black Fork District – Holly Meadows Post Office

House Number 200

Family	Age	Birthplace
Parsons, Job Sr.	66	Virginia
Parsons, Sarah	47	Virginia
Parsons, Jemima E.	22	Virginia
Parsons, Jeannette	20	Virginia
Parsons, Rebecca A.	18	Virginia
Parsons, Lovenia J.	15	Virginia
Parsons, Almira V.	13	Virginia
Parsons, Emeranda	10	Virginia
Parsons, Job C.W.	6	Virginia
Parsons, Paul. H.	2	Virginia
Rummell, Thomas B.	21	Virginia

(Fansler 120)

Job Parsons Sr. is the eldest son of William and Catherine (Stoker) Parsons and grandson of Thomas Parsons Jr. His first marriage was to Jemima Ward on May 25, 1815. (MacCabe 43)

Job's second marriage was to twenty-six-year-old Sarah Losh on September 15, 1836, and they had eight children. The children listed above are from this union. Job Parsons Sr. will be discussed further in this book. (MacCabe 43)

Job Parsons Sr. and Job Parsons Jr. are listed in this book as Senior and Junior because they are named as such in county records and history. But, they are not father and son.

44

Black Fork District – Black Fork Post Office

House Number 214

Family	Age	Birthplace
Parsons, William W.	42	Virginia
Parsons, Hester	38	Virginia
Parsons, Solomon H.	21	Virginia
Parsons, Lucinda	20	Virginia
Parsons, Adonijah	17	Virginia
Parsons, Charles	14	Virginia
Parsons, Swasy	12	Virginia
Parsons, Hannah	10	Virginia
Parsons, Worthington	7	Virginia
Parsons, Mary	6	Virginia
Parsons, William C.	2	Virginia
Parsons, Baba	2mos	Virginia

(Fansler 122)

William Ward Parsons (1818-1866) is the first son of Solomon and Mary (Ward) Parsons and great-grandson of Thomas Parsons Jr. William's first marriage was to Hester Ward (1821-1861) in 1837, and they had ten children, which are listed above. He married Agnes Skidmore on April 9, 1863, and they had two children. (MacCabe 86)

William was born on his father's plantation on the Cheat River in Randolph County. He was left fatherless at fifteen years of age. He and his younger brother, Job Jr., managed the plantation and reared five siblings. William became active in the Methodist Episcopal Church and became a minister. (MacCabe 85)

His homestead, at the foot of Backbone Mountain, had a large house, tall sugar maples, wild grapevines, a cool stream, a bountiful orchid, and strawberries that grew in abundance. His family lived happily there. He died a few years after Agnes, and both are buried on the homestead. (MacCabe 86)

ADONIJAH B. PARSONS

Adonijah B. Parsons (1843-1909) is the second son of William W. and Hester (Ward) Parsons and great-great-grandson of Thomas Parsons Jr. He married Rachel Parsons on December 13, 1868.

Maxwell eulogized Parsons as follows: "Hon. A.B. Parsons stands before the people principally as a land and criminal lawyer, although in chancery practice his business is extensive. He is most successful before a jury. He had studied well the modes of presenting an argument in the most forcible manner, and in this he has hardly an equal and no superiors in this or the neighboring counties.

In his early life he was a farmer and school teacher; but, in 1870, in his twenty-sixth year, he commenced reading law, and was admitted to the bar at St. George in 1872. In 1876 he was elected Prosecuting Attorney and served four years, having succeeded Hon. William Ewin in the office. In 1880 he was instrumental in the organization of the Democratic party in Tucker County. In 1882 he was elected from Tucker and Randolph to the Legislature, by sixty-eight majority over three Democrats and a prominent Republican. The several offices which he has held have not, in a great measure, kept him from his legal profession, although he has filled such offices with honor and ability. Scarcely a case comes before the Court in which he is not a counsel for one side or the other. His practice extends through the courts from the bench of the Justice to the Supreme Court of Appeals of West Virginia..." (200-201)

Parsons was a renowned criminal attorney and, along with five other legal talents, served as the states team in one of the most sensational court battles in West Virginia: State vs. Robert Ward Eastham. Eastham had shot Frank Elmer Thompson, a lumber tycoon, to death at Parsons on March 18, 1897. He was convicted of involuntary manslaughter and sentenced to two years in jail. Eastham escaped and was never recaptured. He died in Washington, Rappahannock County, Virginia, on April 9, 1924. (Fansler 280, 601-603)

JAMES PARSONS

Seven of the Parsons families residing in Tucker County in 1860 were descendents of James Parsons and Nancy (Rust) Parsons. Five sons: William R., Abraham, James R., Andrew B., Thomas S. and two grandsons Jesse and Washington, are listed in the 1860 Census.

James Parsons is the fourth son of Thomas Parsons Jr. and was born October 17, 1772, on the plantation seven miles from Moorefield, Virginia. This land had been in the Parsons family since before the revolution. He attended private schools and chose farming as a trade. On July 3, 1796, he married Nancy (Rust) Parsons, and they had eleven children. Nancy was born in Loudon County, Virginia, on September 4, 1776. (MacCabe 138-140)

James Parsons migrated to western Virginia in the spring of 1800 and settled on a large tract of land that had been pre-empted by his father. At this time the Parsons family possessed all the agricultural land from Holly Meadows to St. George. On this new soil he molded and burned the bricks that were used for the foundation and chimneys of a two-story hewed log dwelling. (MacCabe 138-139)

James was a jovial fellow and generally known as "Uncle Jim." He passed away on August 21, 1859. Nancy died on February 7, 1856, and both are interred in Bethel Cemetery, Holly Meadows, West Virginia. (MacCabe 139-140) (Grave marker, Bethel Cemetery, Holly Meadows, West Virginia)

Chapter V

SQUIRE JOB PARSONS SR.

Job Parsons Sr. and Sarah (Losh) Parsons

Jemima Ward (first marriage)
Married: May 25, 1815
Ten children: Mary (Parsons) Parsons, Emily (Parsons) Parsons, Jacob W., Catherine (Parsons) Johnson, Pheobe Ann (Parsons) Glascock, Solomon, Hannah (Parsons) Poling, Susannah (Parsons) Poling, Adonijah and an infant daughter (MacCabe 43)

Sarah Losh (Second marriage)
Married: September 15, 1836
Eight children: Jemima (Parsons) Fansler, Jeanette (Parsons) Hansford, Rebecca Annis (Parsons) Rummell Bonnifield, Lavina (Parsons) Fansler, Elmira V. (Parsons) Hull, Emma (Parsons) Parsons, Job W. and Paul H (MacCabe 43)

Job Sr. Born June 11, 1789, Hardy County, Virginia
Died December 18, 1883, St. George, West Virginia
(MacCabe 43) (Grave marker, St. George Cemetery, St. George, West Virginia)

Jemima Ward: Born 1795
Died February 4, 1835 (MacCabe 43)

Sarah Losh: Born April 4, 1810
Died September 22, 1902
(Grave marker, St. George Cemetery, St. George, West Virginia)

Job Parsons Sr. lived to be ninety-four years of age. He is the maternal grandfather of Worley Parsons.

Job Parsons Sr. is the eldest son of William and Catherine (Stoker) Parsons. He was born in Hardy County, Virginia, and came to Randolph County, Virginia, with his parents in 1796. Generally known as "Squire Job," he was six feet four inches in height and weighed over 250 pounds, indisputably, a man of fine physique and great fortitude. (MacCabe 42) (Fansler 642)

On June 18, 1812, President James Madison declared war on Great Britain, and Job Parsons, at twenty-three years of age, enlisted in the War of 1812. He served an undetermined time at Fort Meigs, which was built in 1813 on the Maumee River, to protect northwest Ohio and Indiana from British invasion. The fort withstood two invasions, the first in May of 1813, and the second was in July. Both failed, and the British retreated. Job also served in Norfolk, Virginia. While at Norfolk, he became ill with camp fever. His aunt, Mary (Parsons) Hinkle, had him carried to her home, and she nursed him to good health. Job returned to his regiment and continued in that service until the end of the war. (MacCabe 42) (http://www.ohiohistory.org/places/ftmeigs/)

Job married Jemima Ward, daughter of Jacob and Elizabeth (Scott) Ward, and they had ten children. Jemima died two days after the birth of an infant daughter who lived but three months. Job's second wife was Sarah Losh, daughter of Stephen and Sarah (Dashner) Losh. (MacCabe 43) (Fansler 642)

Parsons lived on a plantation in Holly Meadows that he had inherited from his father. One and all were warmly received at the "Job Place." This was a further cause to persecute him during the Civil War, as he kept Yankees and Rebels alike. (Maxwell 483- 484)

Job's last days were spent with his daughter, Emma Parsons, at her home near St. George, West Virginia. Job and Sarah are interred at the St. George Cemetery, St. George, West Virginia. (MacCabe 43)

HANNAHSVILLE SKIRMISH

The Civil War had finally come to Tucker County late in May 1861. When that all-powerful struggle began, the people readily chose their sides between the North and South. They were mostly evenly divided; the Dry Fork area was in a majority for the North, while the St. George area was in a majority for the South. Before long the lines were drawn, and the different fractions became hostile, neighbor against neighbor and family against family. (Fansler 134)

In early June large bodies of Confederates were fortifying themselves in Barbour and Randolph counties. The Yankees had strong forces along the railroad at Rowlesburg. This placed Tucker County between the two armies. (Fansler 135)

Several Tucker men had already volunteered in the Confederate service. Among them were William E. Talbott and the Harper Brothers. William J. Harper was in Preston County and Ezekiel Harper in Barbour County following the Yankee movements. Confederate Home Guards had also been organized; among them were David M. Parsons, Nelson Parsons and Hoy Goff. (Fansler 136)

An independent band of armed guerillas led pro-Union sympathizers in the area. With disdain, Job Parsons Sr. named them "Swamp Dragons" because they hid out in the swamps like dragonflies. Job's title gained favor and the name went down in history. Family and friends called them the "Dry Fork Home Guard." They were formed as a reprisal force to take revenge on those that sympathized with the South. John Snyder was the leader of this group. Committed Union men in Tucker County were Dr. Solomon Parsons, Enoch Minear, and William Corrick. (Fansler 136) (Fansler 189)

By June 1861, the intensity had grown between the Union and Rebel citizens. The official functions of the county had pretty much broken down. The Union fraction, in an effort to obtain control of the offices in Tucker County, proceeded to hold a special election in Hannahsville on June 29, 1861. (Fansler 136)

When it was heard in Rebel camps in Randolph County that the Yankees were holding an election, First Lieutenant Robert A. McChesney was sent into Tucker, with a scouting party of ten mounted men for the purpose of thwarting the proposed election. (Fansler 136)

On the night of June 28, 1861, Lieutenant McChesney and his men arrived at the home of Job Parsons Sr. in Holly Meadows and stayed the night. Job's home, where McChesney spent the last night of his young life, stood on the present-day Carl Hedrick farm. (Fansler, p. 136)

Early the following morning, McChesney and his men departed for St. George, five miles away. There he left two or three of his men and was joined by several of the Home Guard including Nelson Parsons. The group departed for Hannahsville, eight miles further down the Cheat River. (Fansler 136)

Guarding the election at Hannahsville was a detachment of the 16th Ohio Volunteer Infantry under the command of Colonel James Irvine. When they learned that the Confederates were advancing, Captain (first name unknown) Miller, along with several men of his company, dressed in farm clothing that had been confiscated from the surrounding homes, and prepared an ambush. (Fansler 136)

These disguised Union soldiers, with arms hidden under their clothes, stood along the road one-half mile above Hannahsville and feigned to be idle spectators that had assembled to watch the soldiers pass by. They had even gone so far as to arrest Joshua Robinson earlier in the day and force him to participate in the ambush. (Fansler 136)

Unsuspectingly, McChesney and his men rode by. As they proceeded along, they were suddenly attacked from the front by a group of Union troops. Turning back, Captain Miller and his men produced their pistols and opened fire on the Confederates from the rear. Confusion and chaos abounded; they soon found themselves hemmed in between the enemy. (Fansler 137)

"We must cut our way through them!" McChesney shouted, as he drew his sword. Some were able to escape, losing guns and horses as they went, and one man was capable of crossing the Cheat River to safety. (Fansler 137)

McChesney and another soldier, Paxon, charged directly into the Yankees. Several shots were fired. Even though the Confederates had double-barreled shotguns, they were not equal to the Yankees who greatly outnumbered them. (Fansler 137)

Captain Miller shot McChesney in the chest near his heart. Even though severely wounded, he remained on his horse until the animal had its leg shot nearly off. Horse and rider fell together. McChesney fell onto a small log, free of his wounded horse, with his hand grasping the bridle rein, and died immediately. (Fansler 37)

Paxton had been shot, but succeeded in breaking away. He rode a good distance until overcome with weakness that forced him to dismount and hide near the road. Before dark all the men had returned except McChesney and Paxton. It was reported that Lieutenant McChesney had fallen in battle but Paxton was seen riding away. "He's alive and I'm going after him!" declared William Harper. After nightfall, he took off in search of Paxton. Harper found him about three miles beyond Miller Hill, badly injured, and slowly making his way on foot up the road. (Fansler 138)

That same evening, Colonel James Irvine, the Union commander, retrieved McChesney's body, along with his sword and personal belongings, and asked the people of Hannahsville to bury the fallen warrior. (Fansler 138)

Early Sunday morning, on June 30th, Mrs. Abraham Talbott went to Hannahsville seeking permission to obtain McChesney's body. Her request was denied, but she was able to determine the location of the grave. On Sunday night John Auvil, Mr. Talbott, and Peter Bohon went to Hannahsville and brought back the body of McChesney. They traveled by sled as a wagon made too much noise. (Fansler 138)

McChesney was buried in William Ewin's family burial ground near his two-story log home at the mouth of Clover Run. Carpenters of St. George made the casket. A salute was fired over his grave by the Home Guards while the ladies of St. George sang reverently in honor of the young soldier fallen in battle. Lieutenant Robert A. McChesney lost his life precisely one day before his twenty-ninth birthday. (Fansler 138)

Colonel James Irvine afterwards remarked "that when he saw McChesney and Paxton charge the Federal lines so gallantly, he secretly hoped both would escape the hail of bullets being showered around them." He later wrote about McChesney, "he bore himself gallantly, and my sympathies were greatly enlisted for him when he fell. What should have been our common country lost a brave and gallant man." (Fansler 139) (Maxwell 321)

Sometime after the war, Robert McChesney's family came from Virginia and moved him to their home burial place in Brownsburg, Rockbridge County, Virginia. (Fansler 138)

LIEUTENANT ROBERT A. MCCHESNEY, C.S.A.

In 1861, Robert McChesney rode unsuspectingly to his death on the day before his 29th birthday. McChesney was more than six feet two inches in height with a well-knit frame and capable of great endurance. He was one of the finest riders in the Confederate Army where every cavalryman was a splendid horseman. Of commanding mien and eagle eye, he was quick of perception and fearless to a fault. His loud clear voice easily carried from one end of the battlefield to the other. He possessed all the qualities of a dashing cavalier, and had he lived, he might have written his name beside such great cavalrymen as Jeb Stuart and Nathan Bedford Forrest.

Even had he known he was to die, he would have behaved no differently; for he came from a long line of fighting men, men who loved home and country, freedom and liberty, religion and honor. His ancestors had fought with William the Conqueror at the Battle of Hastings and with Cromwell in the American Revolution. His own father had fought in the War of 1812.

The fourth of nine children, First Lt. Robert McChesney was born on June 30, 1832, at the family home "Woodlawn" in Brownsburg, Rockbridge County, Virginia. His father was killed before the last child was born, and Robert stayed home to help his mother with the younger children. A farmer by profession, he received his AB degree in business from Washington College (now Washington and Lee University, Lexington, Virginia). McChesney was leader of the Whig Party in Rockbridge County.

He was commissioned first lieutenant in the Rockbridge County 2nd Dragoons on October 2, 1852. The Dragoons were mustered into service April 21, 1861, and sent to present-day West Virginia.

McChesney was the only officer that attempted to rally his men and bring order out of the confusion and chaos in the evacuation of Philippi, West Virginia, considered the first land battle of the Civil War. At the time of his death on June 29, 1861, he was a member of Captain J. R. McNutt's Company of the 2nd Rockbridge Dragoons that afterward became Company H, 14th Virginia Cavalry of Jenkins' Brigade.

A monument honoring First Lieutenant Robert McChesney is located in Hannahsville on the left side of Route 72, traveling north from Parsons and about nine miles below St. George, West Virginia, on land donated by Eugene and Ruth Bohon, whose ancestors were involved in the battle.

An inscription on a monument to the dead of the Confederate States Army, Arlington National Cemetery, Washington, D.C. reads as follows:

Not for fame or reward,
Not for place or for rank,
Not lured by ambition,
Or goaded by necessity,
But in simple
Obedience to duty
As they understood it,
These men suffered all,
Sacrificed all,
Dared all – and died.

JOB PARSONS TAKEN PRISONER

A Federal force numbering about 100 men came from Grafton into Tucker County on August 13, 1861. Captain George R. Latham of Company B, 2nd Virginia Infantry, was in charge. Their primary purpose for the raid was to obtain mounts for their reorganization as a cavalry regiment. They seized fifteen civilian prisoners, 90 muskets, 150 horses and cattle, and nearly 15,000 rounds of musket ammunition. Many farmers in Holly Meadows suffered the loss of their finest horses, and several of them were taken prisoner, marched away and held for weeks. Among those seized were David Bonnifield, Adam H. Long, John Jones, George M. Nestor, Jesse Parsons, Joseph Parsons, and the aged Job Parsons Sr. (Fansler 191)

It was commonly known that the 72-year-old Job Parsons who lived on top of the hill, below Job's Ford in Holly Meadows, was a sympathizer of the South. When the Civil War began, he had expressed his sentiments by voting for secession, and he had harbored Lieutenant Robert McChesney the night before he was killed. On the evening of October 1861, Job received a report that the Yankees were coming. He knew that he was not safe. (Fansler 192)

Early the following morning, he took his best horses into hiding behind Darkey Knob between Job's Ford and Alum Hill. Scarcely had he reached the place of concealment when the soldiers came down the road. With field glasses they searched every corner of his property. (Fansler 192)

Spying his horses, they made a mad dash for them and met Job Parsons coming down the path with his old trusted rifle, making every effort to conceal it. The "blue coats" confronted him. He threw his rifle to his shoulder and called "Halt!" They were momentarily taken aback and obeyed his command. Enjoying their surprise for a moment, Job said, "Now, I suppose I am your prisoner." (MacCabe 42)

Without delay they disarmed Job Parsons, took him prisoner and captured his horses. They marched him back to his home where they ordered dinner. After dinner they started for Rowlesburg, twenty-five miles away, with Job walking in front of the soldiers who were on horseback. Verbal abuse was exchanged between the men. (Fansler 192-193)

Although he was seventy-two years of age, Job Parsons was a huge rawboned man and as tough as buffalo hide. Job continued to walk along in front of the soldiers until the indignities became more than he could bear. Suddenly, he seized a few stones and hurled them at the nearest rider who leaped from his horse to avoid the blow. Seizing the opportunity to escape, Job mounted the horse and dashed away. But the Yankees rode after him and soon rounded him up. (Fansler 193)

Parsons was taken to Grafton before Brigadier General Benjamin F. Kelley. Boldly, Job Parsons roared that he had fought in the War of 1812 to make America a free land and now that freedom was denied him! The Commanding General was impressed by the homespun mountaineer and without further commotion, paroled him, gave him a horse and told him to go home. (Fansler 193)

REBECCA (PARSONS) RUMMELL BONNIFIELD

Rebecca Annis Parsons is the third daughter of Job Parsons Sr. and Sarah (Losh) Parsons. She was born January 25, 1841, in Randolph County, Virginia. (43)

On November 22, 1860, Rebecca married Thomas B. Rummell, the young Beverly attorney who boarded in her father's residence while he was taking the first census of Tucker County. Rebecca and Thomas had two children.   (MacCabe 77)

Rebecca's first child was born during the Battle of Corrick's Ford on July 13, 1861. She and her sister rode horseback four miles through torrential rain to the mountain home of her aunt. Shortly after arriving, she gave birth to a daughter whom she named Garnett. The child died in October 1864.   (MacCabe 77-78)

When the news reached Rowlesburg in November 1861 that St. George had been captured, a strong force was sent without delay to attack the confederate force that was led by John Daniel Imboden. When they found that Imboden had moved on, they moved up to Abraham Parsons' mill and set up their cannons. The force of Federals that held up at Parsons' mill was considered to be the most malicious Yankees ever to be stationed in Tucker County. They were troops of the 123rd Ohio Infantry, commanded by Captain Horace Kellogg. They had roamed the countryside looting and stealing, committing all sorts of destruction.   (Fansler 203)

One young Ohio volunteer had stolen a saddle and bridle on Dry Fork but was unable to secure a horse. He had returned to Parsons' mill with his loot and was in the course of saddling one of Parsons' horses when two girls stepped out of the house. They were twenty-one-year-old Rebecca (Parsons) Rummell and her thirteen-year-old niece, Virginia Parsons. The girls apprehended the horse and tossed the young fellow among the saw logs that lay in the mill yard. The ridicule of his companions increased his fury so that he rushed back at the girls. But, Rebecca nailed him on the chin and knocked him head over heels. Still not satisfied and encouraged by his cohorts, he rushed Rebecca again. This time she beat him up proper. In utter humiliation, he picked up the saddle and bridle and slithered off. (Fansler 203-204)

Rebecca Parsons and her daughter, Isalina, went to California in 1867 and acquired considerable property in Fresno County. She and Thomas Rummell were divorced. Her second marriage was to Arnold Taylor Bonnifield, son of Gregory and Mary (Taylor) Bonnifield. (MacCabe 78) (Fansler 203)

Chapter VI

CAPTAIN JAMES PARSONS

Captain James Parsons Sr. and Rebecca (Simps) Parsons

Elizabeth (first marriage-maiden name unknown)
Married: Unknown
Two children: James and Diana (Parsons) Hyder
(MacCabe 237, 239)

Rebecca Simps (second marriage)
Married: Unknown
Seven children: Solomon, Isaac, Jonathan, Amanda Molonica
(Parsons) Green, Elizabeth "Betsy," and Rebecca
(MacCabe 239)

James Sr. Born circa 1740, Hampshire County, Virginia
Died 1813: Hardy County, Virginia
(MacCabe 239)

Elizabeth Parsons: Born (unknown)
Died (unknown)

Rebecca Simps: Born (unknown)
Died (unknown)

Captain James Parsons was the second son of Thomas Parsons Sr. and Parthenia (Baldwin) Parsons.

Captain Parsons is the paternal great-great-grandfather of Worley Parsons. (MacCabe 236)

FRENCH AND INDIAN WAR 1754-1763

The French and Indian War was one in a string of wars fought between England and France beginning in the 1600s. Each side hoped to gain dominance in Europe as well as in the various European colonies in Africa, Asia and the Americas. The reason that the French and Indian War erupted in the New World involved the Ohio Country. Both the English and French claimed the land west of the Appalachian Mountains.

Beginning in the 1740s both countries had merchants engaged in the fur trade with the Native Americans in Ohio. In the 1750s each side moved to deny the other access to the Ohio Country. French soldiers captured several English trading posts and built Fort Duquesne (Pittsburgh) to defend their territory from English threats. George Washington, with a small force of Virginia militiamen marched to the Ohio Country to drive the French from the region. Unable to capture Fort Duquesne, Washington retreated a few miles from the fort and built Fort Necessity. On July 3, 1754, a combined force of French soldiers and their native allies overwhelmed Fort Necessity marking the start of the French and Indian War in the New World.

France, along with their Native American allies, succeeded on the battlefield over the next few years. Ohio Country natives had traded with both the English and the French. But most tribes feared the large number of British colonists in North America. They feared that the numbers of white settlers would increase, driving the natives from their land.

English Prime Minister William Pitt determined that the best way to defeat France was to first conquer the French in the New World. The British were able to capture Fort Duquesne in 1758, with the assistance of the colonists. The English captured Fort Niagara and

Quebec in 1759, major French holdings in the New World. When Montreal collapsed in 1760, England held control of France's possessions in North America.

The War continued in Europe, Africa, and Asia for three more years, ending in 1763, with both countries signing the Treaty of Paris. England now owned most of modern-day Canada and all the land between the Atlantic seaboard and the Mississippi River, with the exception of modern-day Florida. However the natives, including those in the Ohio Country, stood ready to defend their territory from the colonists' westward expansion.
(French and Indian war accessed online @
http://www.o i histo ycen al.or/ohc/h story/h n ian/ev n s/fren hwar.sh ml)

FORTS IN HARDY COUNTY

Defensive forts began to be built in earnest early in 1756. Fort Pleasant was the first built, located on the bottomland northeast of the point where Anderson Run flowed into Mudlick Run and on the northeast bank of Mudlick Run. The stockade enclosed about an acre and a half of the ground. The main gate was in the north wall facing the Trough. (MacMaster 38-39)

A settler fort already stood on the South Branch about two miles above Fort Pleasant. This fort was generally known as the Town Fort or Fort Holland due to the many settlers of Dutch origin. (MacMaster 39)

Fort Buttermilk was built early in the spring of 1756. It stood on the east bank of the South Branch about three miles south of the junction of the South Fork and the South Branch. Men of the Virginia Regiment continuously garrisoned Fort Buttermilk through 1758. (MacMaster 39)

About three miles further upstream on the South Branch stood Harness' Fort, built by the Harness family for their own protection. Fort George was a stockade on the east bank of the South Branch, nearly opposite the present site of Petersburg. (MacMaster 39)

In 1757, men of the Virginia Regiment formed the garrison at Powers Mill, located nine miles above Fort Harness, and twelve miles from Fort Buttermilk and twenty miles from Fort Pleasant. Fort Defiance was also located in this neighborhood. There was another fort built on Lunice Creek known as Fort Welton. (MacMaster 39-40)

THE BATTLE OF THE TROUGH

The defensive line of forts and stockades had just begun to take shape when the Indians struck again in much greater numbers. Small bands of warriors slipped between the forts and easily avoided the squads of soldiers and militia looking for them. They fell on isolated settlements all along the frontier. (MacMaster 40)

In the spring of 1756, some fourteen Indians struck without warning on the South Fork of the South Branch of the Potomac. The Indians, led by Delaware Chief Killbuck, attacked John Brake's farmhouse that stood about fifteen miles north of Moorefield. Mr. Brake's pregnant wife and a Mrs. Neff were alone at the time. They carried off the two young married women. Mrs. Brake was killed when she could not keep pace. When they reached the vicinity of Town Fort, about one and a half miles south of Moorefield, Mrs. Neff appeared to be asleep so was left unattended. She was able to escape and safely made her way to the fort.

Eighteen men from Town Fort and possibly some from Fort Buttermilk went in pursuit. They followed a trail that lead down the east bank of the South Branch toward the Indian's main encampment in a deep ravine called the Trough. Noticing how easy it was to follow the Indian trail, the men suspected a trap. As they approached the Trough, they dismounted from their horses and left them on a ridge where they could be easily seen. They attempted to surprise the Indians by making their way down to the ravine under cover. Smoke could be seen from the native's fire at the head of the small stream that ran into the South Branch. Unfortunately, a stray dog that had followed them from the fort startled a rabbit and gave pursuit. His relentless yelping gave away their position. Instead of surrounding the Indian band, they found themselves ambushed.

The battle was fought almost within sight of Fort Pleasant. But, with the South Branch in full spring flood, it is unlikely that the men from Fort Pleasant could have come to their aid. History tells us that the battle was an intense struggle. After two hours of rifle fire and hand-to-hand combat, nearly half of the men and a like number of Indians were dead. Recognizing that they were hopelessly outnumbered, and that reinforcements were not coming, some of the men were forced to cut their way through the enemy to escape. Some leapt into the river; others fell back, still firing, along the bottomland on the east side of the South Branch.

Only sixteen years of age, James Parsons was one of the men who escaped. As he neared Fort Pleasant, he swam the river. Indians chased him right up to the gates of the fort. When he told the story of the battle years later to Felix Renick, he recalled tomahawks whistling by his head as he reached the safety of the fort.
(MacMaster 42) (Battle of the Trough accessed online@ http://www/segenealog.com/westvirginia/wv_county/hdy.htm)

LORD DUNMORE'S WAR 1774

In 1768, the Iroquois Indians and the English signed the Treaty of Fort Stanwix. In this agreement, the Iroquois gave the English all of their lands east and south of the Ohio River. While the Iroquois agreed to give up this land, most Ohio natives did not, including the Delaware, the Mingo and the Shawnee.

Dunmore's War was the result of several conflicts that took place in the spring of 1774, on the Ohio River above the mouth of the Little Kanawha River, between Native Americans, particularly the Shawnee, Miami, and Wyandot and white settlers. Violence erupted as these tribes, especially the Shawnee, tried to drive the colonists back east of the Appalachian Mountains.

Mingo Chief Logan and his hunting party were camped at Yellow Creek on the west bank of the Ohio River near present-day Steubenville. On April 30, some members of the hunting party crossed the river to Baker's tavern for their customary ration of rum. Chief Logan was not among them. When most were fairly intoxicated, a group of settlers, under the leadership of Daniel Greathouse, killed all the natives except for an infant child. At least two of those killed were relatives of Chief Logan. The settlers feared that the natives would surely make war in revenge for the killing of their people and their fears were well founded. Logan retaliated by killing thirteen settlers in western Pennsylvania.

Virginia's Governor John Murray, Earl of Dunmore, received word of the hostilities that commenced at Yellow Creek and other points on the Ohio. In response, he mustered forces for the invasion of the native territories.

Virginia would put two substantial armies in the field against the Indians that summer. One division, recruited along the southern Virginia frontier in Augusta, Botetourt, and Fincastle counties, would travel from Camp Union, present-day Lewisburg, West

Virginia, under Colonel Andrew Lewis, to meet Dunmore at the mouth of the Great Kanawha River.

The other division would move down the Ohio from Fort Pitt under Dunmore's personal command. These were the men of the northern Virginia frontier from Hampshire, Frederick, and Berkeley counties. On June 10, 1774, Lord Dunmore ordered out the Hampshire County militia. (MacMaster 64-65)

Captain James Parsons and Captain John Harness, who had both proven their valor as young men in the French and Indian War would command the contingent from present-day Hardy County Lieutenant Harmonous Alkire, Ensign Robert Cunningham Sergeants Ralph Naylor, Richard Byrns, Charles Myers and Daniel Callihorne were in Captain Parsons' company. (MacMaster 65)

As planned, Lord Dunmore traveled to Fort Pitt and then proceeded with his forces down the Ohio River. On September 30 he arrived at Fort Fincastle that recently had been built at Wheeling by Dunmore's order. The force under Colonel Lewis, eleven hundred strong, proceeded from Camp Union to the headwaters of the Kanawha, and then downriver to the appointed rendezvous at its mouth that they reached on October 6. On October 9, a dispatch was sent to General Lewis informing him that Dunmore was at the mouth of the Hocking River, and that he would proceed directly to the Shawnee towns on the Scioto instead of coming to the mouth of the Kanawha as originally planned. He ordered Lewis to proceed from the mouth of the Kanawha and join him for the advance on the town of Chillicothe on the Little Miami River. (MacMaster 65)

Point Pleasant is the county seat of Mason County, West Virginia situated on the Ohio River and at the mouth of the Kanawha River The Battle of Point Pleasant, the only major engagement in Lord Dunmore's War, was fought there on October 10, 1774. Before General Lewis could break camp, 800 to 1,000 Shawnees and their allies, under Chief Cornstalk, attacked him. The battle raged fiercely throughout the day and resulted in the defeat of the warriors who subsequently retreated across the Ohio. The white men suffered a number of losses in killed and mortally wounded.

Lord Dunmore left a small garrison at Fort Gower at the mouth of the Hocking River and moved his forces to the Scioto Valley. A messenger from Cornstalk met him on his advance with a peace pledge. Dunmore met the Shawnee chiefs at Camp Charlotte in the Scioto Valley and concluded a treaty with them. (MacMaster 65)

For the first time, men from the South Branch had an opportunity to see the Scioto Valley and Pickaway Plains. Felix Renick recalled: "Some of our neighbors, who had served in Dunmore's campaign in 1774, gave accounts of the great beauty and fertility of the western country, and particularly the Scioto Valley, which inspired me with a desire to explore it as early as I could make it convenient." Renick explained that he obtained his information from, "an uncle and two of our nearest neighbors on the south branch, the elder captain Daniel McNeill, and Captain James Parsons, who all served in Dunmore's campaign." (MacMaster 66)

Captain Parsons recalled that Logan and a few other war chiefs of the Shawnee and their Mingo allies did not come in for the treaty making at Camp Charlotte. Parsons was with a small force sent by Dunmore to watch their movements. He and his men were sent to Chillicothe and there learned of the peace treaty. (MacMaster 66)

Lord Dunmore returned to Williamsburg at the end of 1774, as a hero. The Indians gave up all land claims south of the Ohio, including hunting, and returned slaves, horses and other plunder. (http://www.ohiohistorycentral.org/ohc/history/h_indian/events/dunwar.shtml) (http://en.wikipedia.org/wiki/Dunmore's_War) (http://93.1911encyclopedia.org/P/PO/POINT_PLEASANT.htm)

HARDY COUNTY

The steady increase of new settlements made the western counties of Virginia too large to meet the needs of the people that lived there. During October 1777, the Virginia General Assembly adopted a bill that took three new counties, to be called Greenbrier, Rockbridge, and Rockingham, out of Augusta County and extended the boundary of Hampshire County that was already too large. The people had to travel many miles over mountains to attend court or file a legal paper. Many claimed that the great distance involved made it difficult for the militia to muster and drill as frequently as law required. Hence, in May 1784, many citizens asked for a new county with Moorefield as the county seat. (MacMaster 107-108)

Isaac VanMeter introduced a bill in the General Assembly in October 1785, to divide Hampshire County into two distinct counties. Hardy County came into being on February 1, 1786. The justices of the new county were ordered to meet in Moorefield at the home of William Bullitt. They would decide where to locate the courthouse and county seat and build the necessary buildings. Two Hampshire County delegates, Isaac VanMeter and Ralph Humphrey, chose the first justices of the peace and sent a list of names to Governor Patrick Henry for his approval and appointment. (MacMaster, p. 108)

George Stump, Jonathan Parsons (son of Captain James Parsons), James Machir and Adam Fisher served as Hardy County delegates to the Virginia General Assembly through the 1790s. (MacMaster 110)

MOOREFIELD

The October 1777, session of the Virginia General Assembly passed an act creating the town of Moorefield. The General Assembly decreed, "That sixty-two acres of land belonging to the said Conrad Moore, in the most convenient place for a town, be, and the same is hereby vested in Garret Vanmeter, Abel Randall, Moses Hutton, Jacob Reed, Jonathan Heath, Daniel McNeill, and George Renick, gentlemen, trustees, to be by them, or any four of them, laid out into lots of half an acre each, with convenient streets, which shall be and the same is hereby established a town by the name of Moorefield." (MacMaster 111)

The trustees were authorized to sell the lots at public auction for the best price and the money from the sell paid to Conrad Moore or his heirs. The trustees were to give each purchaser a deed for his lot, but the buyers were to hold the lots subject to the condition of building on each a dwelling-house eighteen feet square at least, with a brick or stone chimney, to be finished within two years from the date of sale. If they did not build on the lot, the trustees would again have title to the property and could sell it to someone else, using the money to repair the streets or for any other beneficial purpose. This was the standard established for Virginia towns. (MacMaster 111) Among deeds recorded in the Moorefield Courthouse after Hardy County was established in 1786 were Thomas Parsons, Lot Number 19, and James Parsons, Lot Number 30 and 51. (MacMaster 112)

SOUTH BRANCH MANOR

In 1779, the Virginia General Assembly passed a law to confiscate all property in the state that belonged to British Subjects. When Thomas Lord Fairfax died in December 1781, naturally settlers on the South Branch Manor and other land granted by Lord Fairfax were concerned about their title. (MacMaster, p. 115)

John Marshall, the lawyer for the Fairfax interests, decided to buy the manors from Reverend Denny Martin Fairfax, heir to Lord Fairfax. By 1793, John Marshall, his brother, James Markham Marshall, and their brother-in-law, Raleigh Colston, formed a partnership and purchased the South Branch Manor, two tracts of land, one 54,596 acres and the other 1,550 acres. (MacMaster 117)

Lord Fairfax had made a number of new leases in 1779-1780 for land on South Branch Manor. Among the leases that Lord Fairfax issued in 1779, was Thomas Parsons, 22 acres. Lord Fairfax gave 13 new leases in March 1780 to 11 tenants. Among those was James Parsons, 145 acres. (MacMaster 120)

Leases on the South Branch Manor ran for twenty-one years. This did not give the tenant any real security, especially if he were to make considerable improvements on the land. Many South Branch Manor tenants were men of substance who built fine homes, barns and other farm buildings. Under pressure from the tenants, Lord Fairfax made new leases that gave the tenant the right of reversion. This meant that the land did not automatically come back into the hand of Lord Fairfax or his heirs at the expiration of the lease, the way a tenant farm or other rental property would. The tenant had the right to renew the lease or he could sell or will that right to someone else. Land leases by South Branch Manor tenants in 1779-1780 were not necessarily all the land they held in the manor. South

Branch Manor included some of the richest and most profitable farmland in the Northern Neck. (MacMaster 119-120)

The Reverend Denny Martin Fairfax made new leases in 1790-1791 to fifty tenants on South Branch Manor. Thomas Parsons is listed among those leases. Tracts included in these new leases ranged from Robert Ferguson's 522 acres in the possession of George Harness Jr. in 1801, to Henry Carr's 27 acres. (MacMaster 122)

John Marshall began selling land in South Branch Manor in 1797. The list of deeds over the next few years is a census of those that bought the former Fairfax manor lands. The two surviving rent rolls indicate that all the purchasers were former tenants. Among those listed is James Parsons. South Branch Manor gave permanent ownership of some of the richest land in the state to a number of families identified with the history of Hardy County for more than two centuries. (MacMaster 122-123)

HARDY COUNTY CATTLE COMMERCE

Hardy County included the largest cattle operations anywhere in Virginia in the 1780s, and South Branch Manor was a center of this cattle kingdom. Cattle were the dominant agricultural interest in Hardy County for much more than a century after the first settlements. Their business required large seasonal infusions of cash, as well as extensive ownership of land, labor and livestock. (MacMaster 123-124)

The 1779 Virginia General Assembly levied a three-pence-a-head tax in order to meet the rising costs of the American Revolution. This special tax was renewed in 1781, 1782, and 1784. Much to the delight of cattlemen, the tax was repealed in the 1787 session. During these years, the tax assessors naturally kept accurate statistics on the number of cattle owned, the land, and slaves of every citizen in Hardy County. (MacMaster 124)

Hardy County was the most important beef cattle county in Virginia and one of the most important in the United States as early as 1786. Hardy County tax assessors reported 705 white tithables, half the population of Augusta County. Eighteen taxpayers owned 40 or more cattle and some much more. Another 18 taxpayers owned more than 30 but less than 40 head. Thomas Parsons Jr. paid taxes on 50 or more head of cattle.
(MacMaster 124-125) (Tithe, see following page for definition)

There were other sources of wealth in Hardy County besides cattle. Both sheep and hogs occur regularly in the forty-one inventories of Hardy County residents filed from 1780 to 1790. Tax returns also list the number of horses owned by an individual. The larger farmers frequently owned as many as fifteen or sixteen horses. It was unusual for anyone to have as many as twenty horses in the 1780s and 1790s, but the tax list shows that James Parsons paid taxes on twenty horses in 1781-1782. (MacMaster 130)

Tax List

1781-1782 Personal Property Tax List

The 1781-1782 Hampshire County, Virginia, Personal Property Tax List documents the following for Captain James Parsons and Thomas Parsons.

Name	Tithes	Slaves Above 12	Horses	Cattle
Parsons, James	1	12	20	33
Parsons, Thomas	2	7	12	25

(http://www.ls.net/~newriver/va/hamp1782.htm)
(A tithe or tithables is defined as any male over the age of sixteen years or widow that is head of the family)

SLAVES OF THE PARSONS BROTHERS

In 1782, Jacob Fisher, Christopher Snyder, James Parsons, John Bishop Jr., Jacob Bishop, Daniel McNeill, John Higgins, Elijah Greenwell, John McNeill, James Machir, George Harness, and Adam Neff sent a petition to the Virginia General Assembly complaining about two pieces of recently enacted legislation. During the American Revolution, Virginia adopted an act to prevent the further importation of slaves into the state. It was amended several times in the 1780s to allow slave owners who moved to Virginia from another state to keep their property. In 1790, the General Assembly passed an act for granting relief to persons migrating into this state, giving them more time to register their slaves and take an oath that they had not brought them to Virginia to sell. (MacMaster 133)

The Hardy County petitioners objected that they and other "respectable citizens of the back counties" had brought slaves into Virginia from other states at one time or another, unaware they were doing anything illegal. They suggested the repeal of the original act and a new law imposing a heavy fine on speculators. The General Assembly made no response. (MacMaster 133)

When Hardy County became a separate county in 1786, there were 263 slaves within the boundaries of the county. That year's tax assessment indicated that 176 of these 263 slaves lived in the three districts on the South Branch within the present limits of Hardy County. This part of the county had the largest concentration of beef cattle and included many large farms with exceptionally good soil. Of 38 persons in Hardy County who owned more than 30 head of cattle, 26 owned slaves. Colonel Garrett VanMeter was the largest slave owner in Hardy County. He had 9 adults and 5 children on his place in 1786. (MacMaster 132-133)

Records from 1795, tell us that Jonathan Parsons owned four adult slaves and James Parsons three. Thomas Parsons was among fifteen Hardy County residents who owned two slaves. Slaveholding increased over the next few years. In 1801, James Parsons owned nine adult slaves. (MacMaster 135)

Thomas Parsons Jr., in 1804, bequeathed to his fifth son, Miles, one Negro fellow named David and to his sixth son, Thomas, one Negro fellow named Sampson. The remainder of his Negroes was to be sold when his youngest daughter, Elizabeth, reached the age of sixteen. (MacCabe 22)

James Parsons, in his will of 1811, determined that his Negroes, Sambo, Hannah and Sylvia, were to be given to his wife Rebecca "for and during her natural life." At her death the Negroes were to be sold and the proceeds divided equally among her children. "I give to my son Isaac, a negro boy named Ardon; to Solomon, I give a negro boy named Ise; and to Jonathan, a negro boy named Berry… and to Betsy, I give negroes Sally and Sambo, (son of Isaac); to Amanda Molonica, I gave negroes Vinney and Jerry; and to Rebecca I give negroes Helen and Tom. . ." (MacCabe 237-238)

TUCKER COUNTY INDIANS

Tucker County, West Virginia, is bound by Preston County on the north, on the east by Maryland and Grant County, on the south by Randolph County and on the west by Barbour County. It lies along the valley of the Cheat River and includes the tributaries of that stream for about thirty-five miles north and south and twenty miles east and west. The area of the county is about seven hundred square miles. The territory appears to have been unknown to civilized man until about 1762 or 1763. James Parsons and his brother, Thomas, were the first explorers of Randolph County, Virginia, present-day Tucker County, West Virginia.

We know that Native Americans once made Tucker County their home by their flints, weapons, pottery, graves and trails that are scattered along Cheat River. It is uncertain which tribe inhabited Tucker County. Thomas Jefferson, a recognized authority on the natives, believed the Indians who formerly occupied Tucker County were of the Massawomee Tribe of the Iroquois Nation. Jefferson's father, Peter Jefferson, was among the first white men to travel in Tucker County when he surveyed for Lord Fairfax; he, too, was considered a reliable source of information on Indian history. (Fansler 27, 29)

Perhaps it was the Massawomee, but they were gone when the first white man came. If Indians came within this territory at all, it was only to pass through, hunt for game or fight. We are unable to determine why they departed from this part of the state. War may have exterminated them, or they may have gone on to occupy a better land. (Maxwell 28)

Generally, the Indians that killed people in West Virginia came from Ohio. They had towns on the Muskingum, Tuscarawas, Hockhocking, Scioto, Sandusky, Maumee, Miami, and throughout the intervening country. The meanest Indians were those on the Sandusky and Scioto. (Maxwell 29)

During the winter the Indians lay in their huts by the fire. But, when spring came, they picked up their guns, knives and tomahawks and prepared to raid the settlements. They traveled about twenty miles a day. If they set out from the Scioto River on the first of May, they reached the Ohio somewhere between Point Pleasant and Wheeling in four to seven days. They crossed that river on a raft of logs, and if they were aiming for Cheat River, they reached it from four to seven days longer. (Maxwell 29)

When they came into a settlement, they hid in fence corners and brier thickets until they saw a chance to kill someone. Sometimes they killed, and other times they carried away prisoners. When carrying a prisoner off, they tied his hands and forced him to walk between two warriors. If they had plenty to eat, they fed the prisoner well; but if their provisions were scarce, they gave the prisoner very little. When they got the prisoner to Ohio, they sometimes pummeled him to death with clubs and rocks. Other times they tied him to a tree and burnt him. Occasionally, they adopted him into their tribe and treated him well. A prisoner never knew his fate. (Maxwell 29-30)

CAPTAIN PARSONS DISCOVERS
TUCKER COUNTY

During the French and Indian War, the Indians often moved from beyond the Ohio, across the Allegheny Mountains, and into the settlements along the Potomac River, particularly the South Branch. The Indians killed or carried away many prisoners. On one such raid they captured Captain James Parsons and carried him back to Ohio, keeping him prisoner for some time. (Maxwell 18)

About 1762, Captain Parsons managed to escape from the Indians and headed east toward his home with the sun to guide him by day and the moon by night. Believing that he followed a tributary of the Potomac that would lead him to his home on the South Branch, he continued many days becoming confused. He struck a small river that he reasoned to be the South Branch because it flowed in an easterly direction. But the river did not turn east convincing Captain Parsons that he was following the wrong river. He then left the river, turning eastward across the mountains. Parsons passed Laurel Ridge somewhere near the head of Clover Run and came to Cheat River above Holly Meadows. He then concluded that this must certainly be the South Branch and followed it. His journey took him into the Horseshoe Run area. Captain Parsons was amazed with the beauty of the country, particularly the great forest of white oak trees that covered the entire bottom land of the river from Holly Meadows to the mouth of Horseshoe Run. Nearly all the trees were the same size, with very little underbrush. (Maxwell 18-19)

Up to this time Parsons had thought that this river must surely be the South Branch, but now realized that it was too large. Already it was larger than the South Branch at Moorefield. He realized that he must still be far above that town. Besides, he knew of no country around Moorefield that resembled this area, and if it were the South

Branch, he was above the mouth of both the North and South forks, or upon one of those rivers. Neither was half as large as the Cheat River at Horseshoe. Captain Parsons concluded that this could not be a branch of the Potomac. He was even more convinced when he passed round the high point of the land and saw that the river, instead of continuing toward the north-east, broke away toward the west and flowed in that direction as far as he could see. (Maxwell 19)

Captain Parsons knew of no river of this kind anywhere in the west, and for the first time in all his wanderings, he became truly confused. He would have followed down the river in the hope that it would lead him to some settlement, but he felt sure that it must empty into the Ohio.   (Maxwell 20)

After pondering over the matter for some time, he resolved to continue his eastward course.   Crossing the river at the mouth of Horseshoe Run, Parsons traveled up the stream a short distance coming to a large path. It was most likely an old Indian trail, and he would have followed this had it not turned north. He left Horseshoe Run at the mouth of Leadmine and, by going up Leadmine, crossed the Backbone Mountain near Fairfax.   Captain Parsons struck the North Branch of the Potomac and finally reached home. (Maxwell 21)

FIRST WHITE MEN IN TUCKER COUNTY

According to Fansler, the first white men known to have been in Tucker County were the eight Virginians who made the original survey for Lord Fairfax in 1736. The second forty-man survey team who came along ten years later in 1746, found the year (1736) and their initials carved on four trees at the site of the Fairfax Stone. The names of five were: Benjamin Winslow, William Mayo, J. Savage, Robert Brook and Joshua Fry. The other three men bore the initials FF, BL, and PG. This information was documented in a journal kept by Thomas Lewis, a member of the second surveying team. (47)

Fansler believed that Captain James Parsons was the third white man in Tucker County. It is possible that other whites were captured by the Indians and led through Tucker County or traveled through it while attempting to escape, but there are no records indicating such. (47)

When James Parsons returned to the South Branch after his escape from the Indians in 1762, he gave glowing tales to friends and neighbors of the awe inspiring splendor of the country that he had passed through. But, it was several years before James and his brother, Thomas, returned to the Horseshoe bottom. Maxwell reasoned that it was ten years (1772) before the Parsons brothers traveled back to the Cheat to look over the land and select favorite places. Fansler believed seven years had passed (1769) before they revisited the Horseshoe. But, the Parsons brothers returned and claimed the land. James chose the Horseshoe, and Thomas selected all the land from the mouth of Horseshoe Run to Holly Meadows. Thomas was approximately thirty-nine years of age, and James was twenty-nine.   (Maxwell 32)   (Fansler 53)

JOHN MINEAR

John Minear, a thirty-seven year old immigrant, was born in Germany about 1732, and came to America in 1755. John was fascinated by the tales of Captain Parsons and, in the true frontier spirit, set out for Holly Meadows, arriving the summer of 1773. He visited the country along the Cheat River, selected a suitable farm in the Horseshoe, and returned to the South Branch for his family. (Maxwell 34) (Fansler 55)

John Minear brought along forty or more settlers from the South Branch to the Horseshoe Bend, when he returned in March of 1774. Among those who came with Minear were his two sons, Jonathan and David, his son-in-law Philip Washburn, Salathiel Goff, John T. Goff, Andrew Miller, Henry Miller, Daniel Cameron, Frederick Cooper, Henry Fink, James Riddle, Joseph Hardman, Thomas Holbert, Robert Cunningham and Thomas Parsons. There were many women and children including John Minear's daughter, Elizabeth, who was the wife of Philip Washburn. Thomas Parsons' sister, Prudence, and his daughter, Catherine, also accompanied this group. Prudence was the wife of Robert Cunningham, and Catherine was the wife of John T. Goff. (Fansler 54)

Minear had little difficulty in gathering a group of farmers willing to risk their fortunes for this new land. He was a dynamic leader in whom others easily placed their confidence. John was more educated than his companions, so they looked to him as a military leader in those expected wars with the Indians, and as a counselor in civil affairs pertaining to the settlement of land and deeds. They did not come to the Cheat merely to explore the country; but, they brought with them their families and possessions, with full intention of making it their permanent home. (Maxwell 34-35)

During that year the Dunmore War occurred, when the Indians were defeated and driven back across the Ohio River. But, the danger continued and fear was widespread. Minear's colony built a crude fort near where the county farm buildings are now located and moved into it for their protection. (Fansler 54)

The fort was nothing more than a large log house with holes between the logs through which the settlers could shoot the Indians It was also used as a dwelling for all the families. During the day the men went to the woods to clear cornfields, leaving the women and children in the fort. If an alarm was made, the men ran to the fort and barred the doors, watching through the cracks for the enemy (Maxwell 35)

The Indians continued to raid and murder throughout western Virginia. Frequently, they could be found lurking in the vicinity of the fort. Early in the fall of 1774, the colony gathered their belongings and fled for their homes on the South Branch. (Fansler 54)

John Minear did not return to the Horseshoe in the spring of 1775. What influenced him is unknown. Fansler states that a dispute took place between Minear and the Parsons brothers as to the ownership of the lands in the Horseshoe Bend and Holly Meadows He goes on to say that the dispute was settled by an offer from Minear who gave the Parsons brothers their choice of lands since there was equally good land nearby. James Parsons took the Horseshoe Bend and Thomas the Holly Meadows. Minear selected a site for his colony two miles down the river, where present-day St George is located. (54-55)

On the other hand, Maxwell says that it is well known that a dispute took place between Captain Parsons and John Minear, but the final settlement at the land office gave the Horseshoe lands to Captain Parsons. (39)

FORT MINEAR

We are unsure of the precise number who came to Cheat River in the spring of 1776, when John Minear returned with the colonists. We do know that some of the immigrants who made the trip in 1774 did not return, and that some came in 1776 for the first time. In addition to John Minear and his two sons, David and Jonathan, and several daughters, and other women, there were men named Miller, Cooper, Goff, and Cameron. John Minear did not return to the Horseshoe but moved two miles down the river to St. George, at the mouth of Mill Run. His son, Jonathan, settled on the opposite side of the river. (Maxwell 39-40)

A substantial fort that would offer defense against the Indians was built straight away. The fort stood where the St. George Courthouse was later built and was four times larger than the one built at Horseshoe. (Maxwell 40)

Fansler describes the fort as follows: "Fort Minear, in Saint George, was a two-story log structure, with the logs hewed and mortised so that they fit tightly together, one upon another. The chimney was on the inside and there were no windows, although some portholes were cut in the upper story to admit light and shoot through. Wood blocks were made to fit the portholes so that they could be closed for winter and when otherwise desired. The door was made of puncheon so thick bullets would not pass through. The fort was surrounded by a stockade, a square of heavy posts, planted firmly in the ground, fitted closely together and rising about twelve feet high. The entire enclosure covered over a fourth of an acre. Although forts of this nature appeared to be sturdy enough, they could not withstand a long concentrated Indian attack. If they did not fall by burning or overwhelming numbers, they usually fell when water, food or ammunition became exhausted." (31)

Prior to 1774, the Parsons Brothers had not erected significant homes on the Cheat River. In 1776, when the colony resettled that spring, both Thomas and James Parsons brought sharecroppers with them under contract and began building up their vast estates, but neither remained as permanent settlers. Thomas Parsons Sr. had died in Hardy County in 1772 bequeathing to his sons substantial estates in that county. According to Fansler, the Parsons brothers were "really in the chips." They never lived permanently in Tucker County but maintained their residences in Hardy County, leaving the Cheat River holdings to their sons. (56)

During the first four years, the Minear Colony prospered greatly on the banks of Mill Run. Nevertheless, there was constant anxiety that Indians would invade the settlement. There was less fear in the winter months, as Indians did not travel through the snow. But, when the spring came, West Virginia and Kentucky were overrun with warring reneagades. (Maxwell 41)

The years of 1780 and 1781 were the most devastating in the Indian wars. Randolph County and the more southern counties along the western base of the Alleghenies were well known to the Indians who had passed through them making raids into Virginia during the French and Indian War. Early on, Tucker was secluded; there was no cause for Indians to pass through. If they did so, it was for the purpose of hunting or exploring. Before they could reach Tucker County, they had to pass through several inhabited counties, which the Indians did not like to do as the settlers might track them. In due course, St. George became the most thriving settlement on Cheat River and the Indians soon learned the paths that led to the new country. Tucker's isolated position and its high mountains no longer defended the settlers. (Maxwell 42)

A band of Shawnee Indians crossed the Ohio River, near Parkersburg in March 1780, and raided through the central counties of western Virginia. They avoided the thickly inhabited areas and stayed close to the secluded regions, such as Tucker and Randolph counties. (Maxwell 42)

The Indians made their way unobserved into Lewis County to a fort known as West's Fort. There were only a few men in the fort, and they were terrified to go out and fight the enemy. The people were penned in and soon starving, with Buckhannon the nearest place for assistance, sixteen miles away. One of the captives, Jesse Hughes, was one of the most successful Indian fighters in West Virginia. He had fought the Indians for eleven years and knew them well. His farm was almost within site of the fort and, like his neighbors, he had sought shelter there. It seemed evident that something had to be done, and the most practical plan was sending a man to Buckhannon to bring help. Hughes volunteered to go. On a dark night, he slipped from the fort, evaded the Indians, and ran to Buckhannon. A company of men arrived about daylight and carried the hostages safely to Buckhannon. (Maxwell 42-44)

Thus far, the savages had raided through Lewis and Upshur counties. They then passed into Randolph, where they continued to murder settlers and burn their property. In Tygart Valley they killed John McClain, John Nelson, James Ralston, and Mrs. John Gibson, wounded James Crouch, and captured John Gibson and his children. (Maxwell 45) (Fansler 30)

The settlers had made it though the bitter winter, but it had been a severe one for Minear's colony. In addition to suffering from hunger, the smallpox broke out, and it fell heavily on the indigent settlers. (Maxwell 48)

In early spring, the Indians moved from the Tygart Valley, down the Cheat River, toward St. George. But the news of the Indians had preceded them, and the settlers along the Cheat River had left their cabins and moved into Fort Minear. (Fansler 30)

BERNARD SIMS MURDERED

 Those families who had one or more members with smallpox were not permitted to move into Fort Minear. This was a difficult resolution to be made, but it was decisively better for a few to risk the Indians than for the entire colony to be stricken with smallpox. (Fansler 30)

The family of Bernard Sims was among those barred. Thomas Parsons had brought Sims to the area as a tenant farmer, and he was living in a log cabin on the upper part of Thomas Parsons' land, about three miles above Fort Minear. One of James Parsons' old Negro slaves, the mother of fifteen children, was working for and living with the Sims family. (Fansler 30)

On April 6, 1780, the Indians left Tygart's Valley and aimed for St. George. Passing along the west bank of Cheat River, from the mouth of Pleasant Run, known locally as Pheasant Run, they arrived within a few miles of the fort when they came into the clearing at Sims' cabin. The Indians made their way, through the tall grass, warily crawling toward the house, when the Negro woman spotted them. She ran to the door and gave the alarm. Bernard Sims, recovering from smallpox, seized his rifle and ran outside. As he stepped into the yard, an Indian shot him down and rushed forward to scalp the dead man. When the Indians observed the dreaded smallpox, they ran from the yard yelling, "Smallpox! Smallpox!" (Fansler 30)

According to Maxwell, Sims was brought to the Cheat by Captain Parsons, and was a tenant on the Parsons' land. He had been placed on the farm where he was killed, to oversee the upper part of James Parsons' land, and to keep Thomas Parsons' cattle from crossing over into the Horseshoe. (48)

After killing Sims, the Indians moved down the river and concealed themselves on a ridge on the opposite side, overlooking the fort. The savages waited and watched. Several of the men of the fort were away. Some had been kept away due to smallpox, and others had traveled to Winchester to fetch supplies and had not yet returned. The settlers feared the Indians would attack while the fort was defenseless. The Indians numbered about fifty and if an attack had been made, it is doubtful the fort could have held. To create the impression that the fort was heavily occupied, the garrison dressed in different clothes and paraded about the fort in full view of the Indians. The Indians must have been fooled, because they soon disappeared from the ridge. The men returned from Winchester the following day. When the settlers felt that it was safe and returned to their cabins, they found that the Indians had raided and destroyed many of their possessions. (Maxwell 50-51)

A day or two passed and nothing more was seen or heard of the Indians. But, they had only moved farther down the river about a mile from the fort and selected a new hiding place just above the mouth of Clover Run. (Fansler 31)

JONATHAN MINEAR MURDERED

Jonathan Minear's farm was located two miles below St. George on the south side of the river at the mouth of Lower Jonathan Run. When the Indians first came into the area, he abandoned his farm and retired to the fort. After one or two days with no sign of the Indians, Minear decided to return to his farm and look after his stock. At daylight, on April 16, 1780, Minear and his brother-in-law, Philip Washburn, left the fort and proceeded to the ford, approximately a half-mile below. They met up with Daniel Cameron, who was afoot and on his way to his own farm that was located on the north side of the river opposite Miller Hill. They talked a few minutes and separated. Minear and Washburn crossed the river, and Cameron proceeded down the northern bank. (Fansler 31-32)

When they arrived at Minear's cabin, Washburn went to feed the cattle, and Minear went to get corn for the hogs. Washburn was passing through the bars, with a shock of fodder on his back, when Indians leaped from a fence corner and seized him. Immediately, shots were fired. Minear ran as though wounded toward the river with a dozen Indians chasing after him. He had been shot in the thigh and the Indians were gaining fast upon him. They overtook him at a beech tree near the river. (Fansler 32)

Minear circled the tree in an effort to escape, holding on with one hand and fighting the Indians off with the other. They hacked at him with their tomahawks, severing three of his fingers, as he tried in vain to ward off their blows. There were times they missed him, leaving scars on the tree that remained for 177 years. But, the fatal blows came and Jonathan fell. (Fansler 32)

Washburn stood terrified, with the fodder still on his back, as he watched the murder of Minear. He forgot that he, too, was a prisoner until an Indian ordered him to throw the fodder down. Cameron was watching from the other side of the river, and in the confusion, believed Washburn as well as Minear was dead. He broke and ran for the fort. (Maxwell 54-55)

When they heard the shots at the fort, several men mounted horses and rushed off to investigate. They met up with Cameron who was exhausted from running and could barely speak. He told them that Minear and Washburn were killed. The party halted and talked among themselves. Fearing an ambush and an attack on the fort, and not knowing the strength of the Indians, the men decided to return to the fort and prepare to defend it. (Fansler 32)

The day passed and there was no attack. The next morning, the men gathered from above and below St. George to visit the scene of the tragedy. When they reached a point opposite of where Jonathan Minear was killed, they arranged themselves in a line along the side of the hill. A large Negro named Moats was sent across the river to search the property for Indians. After he searched the thickets and determined that savages were not in the vicinity, the men crossed the river. (Fansler 32-33)

Minear was found lying dead by the beech tree and watched over by his faithful dog. The men searched the woods and cornfields thoroughly, but could find no trace of Washburn. Finally, they saw a trail leading up a ridge, and by following it, they discovered among the moccasin tracts that Washburn had been taken prisoner. The men decided they would follow the trail once Minear was taken back to the fort and buried. (Fansler 33)

The following day, those men that could be spared from the fort took off and trailed the Indians for two days, locating their camp at nightfall. The men rushed into the camp as the savages bounded away in all directions. Several Indians were wounded or killed, and Washburn was rescued unscathed. (Fansler 33)

MINEAR, COOPER AND CAMERON MURDERED

The St. George settlers had improved valuable land without title papers. The Virginia General Assembly had passed an Act that provided for validating all claims to land that had been settled prior to January 1, 1778. Commissioners had been appointed to adjust these claims and execute the legal documents pertaining to claims and claimants. The people in St. George sent John Minear, Daniel Cameron, Andrew Miller, Henry Miller, Fredrick Cooper, and Salathiel Goff to present their claims in Clarksburg. (Fansler 34-35)

On April 5, 1781, the party had obtained the deeds for their lands and was returning from Clarksburg. The Indians had prepared an ambush near the mouth of Hacker Creek in Barbour County. A leather gun-case had been hung over the trail and the Indians were positioned in the thickets on both sides. The party approached, riding single file with Minear in the lead. He was almost beneath the decoy when he saw it and drew back the reins. Realizing an ambush, Minear yelled, "Indians! Indians!" But, it was too late, and the firing commenced. Minear, Cameron and Cooper fell, horses and men together. They lay dead on the trail. Andrew Miller and Goff were unhorsed by now and took off running for the woods. Henry Miller, who had been riding in the rear, turned and beat it back to Clarksburg. (Fansler 35-36)

Salathiel Goff ran for the river in the opposite direction from Miller, with several Indians closing in on him. At the riverbank, he threw off his coat and prepared to swim. Thinking that it would be useless to do so, he threw the coat into the river and crawled into a nearby otter den. When the Indians reached the bank above and saw his coat floating down the river, they moved along keeping pace with it. As soon as they were out of sight, Goff crawled out and headed for St. George, thirty miles away. He reached the fort at nightfall carrying the startling news of the murders. (Fansler 36)

The yelping Indians ran after Andrew Miller with knives and tomahawks in hand. But, he was able to outdistance them and return safely to the fort. (Fansler 36)

When it was learned at St. George that Minear, Cameron, and Cooper had been killed, the settlers proceeded to Hackers Creek to bury the dead. They moved with caution, not knowing where the Indians had gone. When they reached the scene, Minear, Cooper and Cameron were found lying on the trail where the Indians had scalped and left them. They were hastily buried in the nearby root-hole of a fallen tree. It would have been impossible to horseback them over the narrow trail to St. George, not knowing the whereabouts of the Indians. (Fansler 38) Fifteen years of Indian wars ended in Tucker County in 1781.

WILL OF CAPTAIN JAMES PARSONS

In the name of God, Amen. I, Captain James Parsons, of Hardy County and state of Virginia, being advanced to considerable age, but of sound mind and memory do this day of July, in the year of One Thousand Eight Hundred and Eleven, make and publish this last will and testament in the following manner. I give and bequeath to my affectionate wife, Rebecca Parsons, my dwelling house and all out houses and the furniture with the conveniences thereunto belonging, and one-half of my home place with the Negroes Sambo, Hannah and Sylvia for and during her natural life, and I direct my said wife to clothe, school and support her daughters by me until they marry, and Jonathan until he arrives at the age of twenty-one; only all this I give to my wife and at her death I do request that all the Negroes and any property of any description may be disposed of and the proceeds divided equally amongst her children by me. I give and bequeath to my three sons Isaac, Solomon and Jonathan Parsons, (sons of my wife Rebecca) all my lands on the Cheat river, known by the name of the Horse Shoe bottom, agreeable to a division and boundaries already made by me and known to them, and I give to my son Isaac, a Negro boy named Ardon; to Solomon, I give a Negro boy named Ise; and to Jonathan, a Negro boy named Berry, all this I give to my said sons and theirs forever. I give and bequeath to my daughters, Betsy, Amanda Molonica, and Rebecca Parsons, one thousand dollars each, to be paid to them out of my home place by my son James Parsons when they arrive at twenty-one years and to their heirs; and to Betsy, I give Negroes Sally and Sambo, (son of Isaac); to Amanda Molonica, I gave Negroes Vinney and Jerry; and to Rebecca I give Negroes Helen and Tom; all this I bequeath to my three daughters and their heirs forever. I give and bequeath to my son James Parsons, my home plantation subject to the above bequests, and should his mother die before his sisters marry or his brother Jonathan arrives at age, I do subject my said son to all the provisions made incumbent on his mother for their support, and I give my said son James, all out surveys and all property not willed or bequeathed and all debts due me, and subject him my said son to the payments of all my just debts and funeral expenses, and direct that all property undivided or willed, be disposed of for this purpose, and the surplus if any to be his, or a deficiency to be made good by him. I do hereby constitute and appoint my wife Rebecca and my son Isaac executrix and executor of my will and testament with full and complete power to make all necessary conveyances of property to be disposed of, and do all things to effect this purpose in an ample manner. All this I confide to my wife and son, not doubting their endeavors in the execution. To this my last will and testament I set my hand and seal this 25th day of July and year above written, and exclude all my children of my former marriage from any participation, having already given them more than the present family possess, and I also exclude my daughter, Dinna Hider, and her husband Michael Hider, from any part, having given them six hundred and twenty pounds already.

Done in the presence of witnesses and signed, sealed, published and declare by the testator as and for his last will and testament who at his request and in his presence and in the presence of each other, subscribed our names, George Harness, Sam McMechin, James Machie.

At a court held for Hardy County, the 13th day of April 1813. This last will and testament of James Parsons, deceased, was produced in Court by Rebecca Parsons and Isaac Parsons, the executrix and executor named therein, provided by the oaths of George Harness, Jr., Samuel McMechin and James Machie, the witnesses thereto, and ordered to be recorded, and on the motion of the said Rebecca Parsons and Isaac Parsons certificate is granted them for obtaining a probate thereof in due form, they having taken the oath of an executor, and together with James Machie and James Parsons, their securities, entered into and acknowledge a bond in the penalty of six thousand dollars, conditioned as the law directs.
Ed. Williams, C.H.C.
A Copy, Teste. Ed Williams, C.H.C.
(MacCabe 237-239)

THE CAPTAIN JAMES PARSONS HOUSE

Moorefield, West Virginia

The Parsons House is one of the oldest, if not the oldest, extant structures in Moorefield, West Virginia.   On August 10, 1786, Captain James Parsons paid forty shillings to the trustees of Moorefield for Lot 30. One of the conditions of the deed required Parsons to build a dwelling to be "18 foot square with a stone or brick chimney."

The house is a survivor of more than three centuries of wear and tear, including artillery exchanges between the North and South in the Civil War. It was completely untouched by six major floods that ravaged Moorefield.

Built of heartwood pine, the Parsons house appears to have been built in two stages, the north part being three stories high and the exact dimensions required by the deed. The Parsons family lived in this log house until 1809, when it was sold to John H. Smith. It has changed hands many times since. (See deed that follows)

Over the years, plaster walls and whitewash disguised the original log construction. By 1985, the house was in such disrepair that tearing down the house was being considered. When a hole was drilled into one of the walls, the original log under structure was discovered. Richard and Mary Low Bass spent two years restoring the logs, floor, fireplaces and beamed ceilings. In 1977, the owners Stephen and Dr. Elizabeth Smith restored the German siding on the exterior.

During the restoration of a first-floor fireplace, a letter was found from Kate P. to her friend Rebecca Sangster of Harrisonburg describing the occupation of the town by the "Yankees" during the Civil War. (http://www.heritageweekend.com/moorefield.html)

DEED

James Parsons to John Smith 1809

James Parsons and wife, Rebeckah to John M. Smith
March 10, 1809 (House in Moorefield)

This Indenture made and entered into this 10th day of March in the year one thousand eight hundred and nine between James Parsons and his wife of the one part and John M. Smith of the other part. Both of the County of Hardy. Witnesseth that the said James Parsons for and in consideration of the sum of one hundred pounds warrant money of Virginia to him in hand and secured to be paid the receipt whereof is hereby acknowledged and thereof due forever acquit and discharge the said John M. Smith his heirs Excrs (?) and assigns have granted, bargained, sold Aliened inpeoffed (?) and conveyed and by these presents do grant, bargain, sell, alien enfeoff (?) and convey unto the said John M. Smith and his heirs forever a certain tract, piece or parcel of land containing half an acre in the town of Moorefield, in the said County of Hardy on the back street nearly opposite the Meeting House and bounded on the north east by the Lott at present occupied by Jones Green and appartaining to the Tavern on the south east by the said back street which divides it from the said Meeting House or place of public worship on the south west by the vacant Lott of Samuel W. Mechum Esqs. Purchased of Cuthbert Buttitt of the State of Kentucky on the north west by W. Edward Williams Lott on which his brick house stands and is known and distinguished in the place of the said Town by Lott No. now in the possession and occupation of Alexander Wallace Esqs. and all houses and out houses, garden, and appertenances thereunto belonging or in anywise appertaining or therewith held occupied used or enjoyed or parcel of the same to the said John M. Smith his heirs and assigns to the only proper use and be hoof him the said John M. Smith his heirs and assigns forever and the said James Parsons his wife for themselves and his heirs the title of the aforesaid lot of land and houses and appertenances to the said John M. Smith and his heirs and assigns against the claim of heirs and the said James Parsons his wife and their heirs and all and every person or persons whatsoever shall and will forever warrant and defend. In witness whereof the said James Parsons his wife have hereunto set their hands and affixed his seal the day and year above written. (http://www.rootsweb.com/~wvhardy/pars1809.htm)

Chapter VII

SOLOMON PARSONS, M.D.

Solomon Parsons, MD and Hannah (Parsons) Parsons

Married: August 20, 1810
Three children: Diana (Parsons) Parsons, James William, and
Rebecca (Parsons) Elliott
(MacCabe 241)

Solomon Parsons: Born October 13, 1795, Hampshire County,
Virginia
Died November 15, 1875, Preston County, West Virginia
(MacCabe 241)

Hannah Parsons: Born March 14, 1791, Hardy County, Virginia
Died January 29, 1871, Preston County, West Virginia
(Grave marker, Maplewood Cemetery, Kingwood, West Virginia)

Dr. Solomon Parsons, son of Captain James Parsons, is the paternal
great-grandfather of Worley Parsons. Hannah (Parsons) Parsons,
granddaughter of Thomas Parsons Jr., is Worley's paternal great-
grandmother.

D r. Solomon Parsons is the son of Captain James Parsons and his second wife, Rebecca Simps, and grandson of Thomas Parsons Sr. Solomon was born on the James Parsons plantation in Hampshire County, Virginia. He received his education from the finest schools in Romney, graduated from a medical college in New York, and was a licensed physician. (MacCabe 240)

Along with his brothers, Isaac and Jonathan, Solomon inherited from Captain Parsons all his land on the Cheat River known as the Horseshoe bottom. It is uncertain when Solomon settled in the Horseshoe; but he began his medical practice soon after moving to present-day Tucker County. Dr. Parsons also owned and managed a general merchandise store near St. George. (MacCabe 237, 240) (Fansler 196)

Much of Solomon's effort was directed to the cause of social reform. When the slave question surfaced, he took a firm stand and gave his Negro "Ise" emancipation. He was equally devoted toward the building of quality schools so that his children could have a good education. Solomon was most dedicated to the "good work," and he encouraged others to do the same. Perhaps to him, more than any other is due the building of the Ann Eliza Church (St. George United Methodist Church) that is situated along Mill Run and continues to hold regular weekly services even today. Solomon and Hannah were members of the Methodist Episcopal Church for sixty years. (MacCabe 238, 240)

Dr. Parsons was a strong Union man, having been a Whig; but he became a staunch Republican when that party was organized. He heartily supported all its candidates and principles. (MacCabe 240)

Solomon retired from active business in 1863 and moved to Terra Alta, Preston County, West Virginia, where he died. He and Hannah are interred in the Maplewood Cemetery, Kingwood, West Virginia.

DIANA (PARSONS) PARSONS

Diana Parsons (1811-1876), daughter of Dr. Solomon Parsons and Hannah, was born in the Horseshoe. She married John Rust Parsons (1806-1882), the fourth son of James and Nancy (Rust Parsons, and grandson of Thomas Parsons Jr., on December 11 1827. Diana and John are the parents of thirteen children. (MacCabe 172-173)

John built a comfortable log home in the Horseshoe, and they lived there for ten years. But in the spring of 1837, several explorers, included the Parsonses, formed a wagon train and migrated to Jefferson County, Iowa. John and Diana settled on a large tract of land and built a cabin that was later replaced with a brick home. Parsons prospered in the stock business and held a number of public offices, including justice of the peace, an office he held for ten years. For many years Diana was the only doctor in the community. She was well-read on medicine and assisted with several childbirths. They were devoted parents, and as their children married, they purchased land and settled them close by. A village sprang to life around them, which was named "Parsonsville." (MacCabe 172-173)

Diana told many interesting stories about her pioneer life. I appears that an Indian village was not far from where they lived. She and John were curious about the lifestyle of the Indians, so one afternoon they called upon them. The cook was boiling a big turtle with corn. A pressing invitation was extended to have some dinner But they politely excused themselves and hurried off. (MacCabe 173)

Diana traveled often to West Virginia to visit family and friends. On one such visit, she passed away suddenly at the home of her son on August 28, 1876. John lived another six years and passed away on November 27, 1882. (MacCabe 172-173)

PARSONSVILLE PASSES INTO
COUNTY HISTORY

The following is a newspaper article taken from the *Fairfield Ledger*, about 1952. It is an account of the founders of Parsonsville, Iowa, John Rust Parsons and Diana (Parsons) Parsons:

When fire destroyed the Nova Harper home about seven miles east of Fairfield last week, it wiped out the last remaining structure that was once the thriving community of Parsonsville.

During the peak of its existence the little village included one or two stories, a tavern, a blacksmith shop, a Methodist church and several homes.

The village was settled by John Rust Parsons, who was born Nov. 22, 1806, in Tucker County, West Virginia. After his marriage he and his wife and family started west toward Iowa in 1836. They traveled in a wagon drawn by six or eight yoke of oxen.

When cold weather set in, they remained during the winter months at Cairo, Ill. They continued their journey the following year, arriving in this area in 1837.

Just why they chose Parsonsville for their home has not been recorded. The territory at that time was all government land, and free for settling at a $1.25 per acre. After staking a claim, which included several hundred acres, Parsons built a log cabin. Much of the area was timber at that time. He cleared the land and a few years later built another log house.

That log house is now part of the house on what is known as the Bush farm. In later years when the house was enlarged, the cabin became the kitchen and it was covered with weather boarding on the outside, and plastered inside. The place is now owned by the Will

Bush estate and is located about a quarter of a mile north of the Parsonsville corner on highway 34.

That is actually the last remaining part of the original Parsonsville, but it is so disguised now that one would never know that the kitchen part of the house is made of logs.

The home that burned recently was originally the old Soloman Nelson home, and one of the several homes erected in the village.

As more and more people settled in and near the little community, there was need for a place of worship. Until 1874 all religious gatherings were held in the schoolhouse.

During the year 1874 Parsons took the lead in erecting a church. Others who played an important part in the establishment of the church included George and Martha White, James H. Hendricks, F.S. Toothacre, Diana Parsons, Elizabeth Shoemaker, R. Toothacre, Baldwin Parsons, Benjamin Archibald, N. C. C. Lindstrom, Loren Clark, Hiram Heaton and John Steward.

Parsons furnished all the dimension lumber and most of the labor was donated. As a result the church was built at a minimum cost.

Shortly after the church was completed, it was announced at a meeting that it lacked only one hundred dollars of being paid for. Mrs. Parsons reached down in the large pocket of her dress, brought forth the $100, and commented, "There, now that will our church of all debt."

Finally, the little community dwindled, its members vanished, and the church was no longer active. It remained idle for several years and the church building was sold at auction in November 1952. It was then torn down.

The church was located a short distance east of the house that burned last week. The lane going back to the house was once the main road now known as Highway 34.

Parsons is also credited with locating Highway 34 from Parsonsville to Fairfield. He didn't locate the route with surveyor's instruments, but marked the route with a plow and a yoke of oxen.

That was in the early 1840's when Fairfield was yet a tiny village. Information states that Parsons took four yoke of oxen, attached them to a huge breaking plow and thus "blazed the trail to Fairfield" by one continuous furrow.

It is said that oftentimes the driver couldn't see the front yoke of oxen on account of the large amount of prairie grass, which grew from six to eight feet tall. It is estimated it took two days for the slow oxen to make the trip.

That trail is now the newly paved Highway 34, and its route has been changed very little since it was originally marked by the plow.

While the highway still remains, the little community of Parsonsville has now disappeared. It has passed from existence as several other early communities have done.
(Courtesy of Marvin E. Parsons)

JOHN RUST PARSONS

Obituary
Fairfield Ledger
December 2, 1882

A Pioneer Gone

The funeral of another of Jefferson County's pioneers occurred yesterday afternoon – that of Mr. John R. Parsons. He died at his home in Buchanan Township Monday evening. For many years Mr. Parsons had suffered from a fever sore on one of his legs, and several weeks ago was taken with crysipelas (erysipelas). Later gangrene set in and prevailed throughout his whole system, finally causing his death.

Mr. Parsons was a native of Randolph County, West Virginia, where he was born December 2d, 1806. His wife was Miss Diana Parsons. She, too, was a native of the same County, where they were married Dec. 11, 1827. Mrs. Parsons died in August 1876.

To Mr. And Mrs. Parsons thirteen children were born, all but two of them reached the age of manhood, and most of them still reside in this County. Mr. And Mrs. Parsons came to this County in 1837, settling, we believe, on the land, which is now a part of the large farm on which they lived so many years. Quite a number of our people fathered around them and in time quite a village, "Parsonsville," named after the family, flourished near the home. They endured together the hardships of pioneer life, and enjoyed together the happinesses of prosperity and civilization, and during their life gathered quite a share of this world's goods, the homestead recently embracing a tract or nearly five hundred acres of land.

Mr. Parsons was a democrat in politics and when that party was in power in this County held a number of minor offices. He first resided in what was known as the "Brush Creek" election precinct, composing what is now Lockridge and Buchanan Townships, and when Buchanan Township was organized he was its first justice of the peace, an office he held for ten years or more. He was also a member of the jury at the first regular term of court held in this county.

He was a man who was generally esteemed by his fellow men; generous and hospitable to his friends, and who possessed a store of recollections of Iowa pioneer life.
(Courtesy of Marvin E. Parsons)

James Parsons 1772-1859
From MacCabe's Parsons
Family History and Record

Jesse Parsons 1825-1896
From Fansler's History of
Tucker County West Virginia

Job Parsons, Sr. 1789-1883
From MacCabe's Parsons
Family History and Record

Rebecca (Parsons) Bonnifield
1841-Unknown
From Fansler's History of
Tucker County West Virginia

Abraham Parsons 1809-1884
From MacCabe's Parsons
Family History and Record

Emily (Parsons) Parsons 1817-1898
From MacCabe's Parsons
Family History and Record

Ward Parsons 1827-1898
From MacCabe's Parsons
Family History and Record

Sarah (Parsons) Parsons 1828-1910
From MacCabe's Parsons
Family History and Record

Tucker County Courthouse, St. George, West Virginia (1858-1893) The men appearing above are *left to right*: Cyrus Haymond Maxwell, Adonijah B. Parsons (1843-1909), Wilson Bonnifield Maxwell, Adam Harper Wamsley, Luke Gregory Bonnifield, Arnold Allen Henry Bonnifield, Will Edgar Cupp, Lloyd Hansford, Creed Wilbur Minear, Lorenzo Sydney Auvil, William M. Cayton, George Francis Griffith and Henry W. Dumire.

The Captain James Parsons House
Moorefield, West Virginia Circa 1786

St. George Academy 1886-1893
St. George, West Virginia

St. George United Methodist Church Circa 1840
St. George, West Virginia

Mob Moving the County Records on Main Street
Parsons, West Virginia 1893

Mob Moving the County Records on Second Street
Parsons, West Virginia 1893

Solomon John Parsons Family *left to right*
Marvin Parsons, Solomon J. Parsons, Worley Parsons, Emma (Parsons) Parsons
and Hattie (Parsons) Hahn

Gathering at the Solomon J. Parsons House
St. George, West Virginia, about 1901

First from left on top row is Harriet (Parsons) Long, daughter of Abraham Parsons. Emma (Parsons) Parsons is standing fourth from left with her sister, Jemima (Parsons) Fansler. William T. Hahn and wife, Hattie (Parsons) Hahn, are standing eighth and ninth from left. Solomon J. Parsons is seated second from left with a child, Marie Hahn. Next to Solomon is the aged Sarah (Losh) Parsons, widow of Job Parsons, Sr. Seated on Sarah's left is her daughter, Rebecca (Parsons) Rummell Bonnifield with a child. Seated third on Sarah's left is Marvin Parsons, son of Solomon and Emma Parsons, and his wife, Amy (Lipscomb) Parsons, standing to his left holding a child. Others that attended what was believed to be an anniversary party were Mr. and Mrs. John J. Adams, Mr. James Long, Mrs. William E. Talbott and son Paul, David S. Minear, Mary Cupp, wife of William E. Cupp, Lace Long with two sons, Anna Baughman, Addie Adams Strieby, Mabel Talbott, Marie (Cupp) Nestor, Clara Adams Peck and Jeckie Adams. Some could not be identified.

Olive Marie Hahn 1899-unknown and James M. Parsons

Amy M. (Lipscomb) Parsons 1879-1954 and Marvin Parsons 1879-1964

Parsons Family Reunion held in the Holly Meadows
August 21, 1909

Worley Parsons about fourteen years of age

Solomon Parsons 1848-1926
with grandchildren
Margaret (Halfin) Parsons *left*
and James E. Parsons

Worley Parsons four years of age

St. George School
St. George, West Virginia
Worley Parsons *back row, third from left*

St. George School, St. George, West Virginia
Worley Parsons *back row, third from left*

Parsons Family Reunion (date unknown)
Worley Parsons *back row, third from left*

Worley Parsons 1886-1972

Worley Parsons on the Parsons Farm

Worley Parsons' Saw Mill on Dry Run
St. George, West Virginia

Worley Parsons 1886-1972

St. George Baseball Team, Carl Close, Elie Pifer, Maurice Parsons, Fred Parsons, Chet Close, Frank Barr, Otis Barr and others. Worley Parsons, Manager

Worley Parsons was known as an avid fisherman. On rare evenings, after the chores were completed on the farm, he sauntered through the fields to the Cheat River below. It was on the Cheat that he caught this bass that measured twenty-eight inches and weighed nine pounds.

Parsons Brothers *left to right*
Marvin, Wilbur and Worley

Worley and Eva (Metz) Parsons with granddaughter,
Carol (Gordon) Carter

Elias Metz 1826- unknown and Minerva J. (Brookover) Metz
Paternal grandparents of Eva (Metz) Parsons

Jefferson Davis Metz and
Amelia (Poling) Metz
Parents of Eva (Metz) Parsons
left

Amelia (Poling) Metz
below

Sisters, Eva (Metz) Parsons *standing*
and Ida (Metz) Arbogast

Four generations: Amelia (Poling) Metz, Eva (Metz) Parsons, James E. Parsons and son, James M. Parsons *top right*

Eva Lena (Metz) Parsons *top left and bottom*

Eva (Metz) Parsons with granddaughter, Carol (Gordon) Carter

James Everett Parsons and Margaret (Parsons) Halfin

James Everett Parsons bottom right

St. George School April 23, 1929
James E. Parsons *third row from bottom, fifth from left*
Margaret (Parsons) Halfin *back row wearing hat*
Clara Ball, Teacher

Margaret (Parsons) Halfin 1916-2006

Robert Floyd Halfin 1917-1996

James Everett Parsons 1918-1972

James E. Parsons *top left*
James E. Parsons *top right on left* and Arthur Barr

1938 Parsons High School Parsons Panthers
James E. Parsons *first row, third from left*

The Parsons Echo

DEVOTED TO THE INTERESTS OF PARSONS HIGH SCHOOL

PARSONS HIGH SCHOOL, PARSONS, W. VA., NOVEMBER 28, 1938.

R REGIONAL PRESIDENT E. F. F. A. SCHOOL GROUPS

SEVEN MEMBERS OF THE 1938 FOOTBALL TEAM

SCHOOL BOND ISSUE OF CO PASSES WITH NEEDED

TOP ROW, left to right:— Mont Wratchford. Elwood Riley, Arthur Barr, Neil Ball.

LOWER ROW, left to right: —James Parsons, Virgil Barr, Carlton Bennett, Odford Gray, Manager.

COACH MYRL KEPNER

Don Garber Donates Old Edition Of Echo

It Did Happen Here! America Cannot Rest

Commercial Club Has Expert Typist To Demonstrate

The Parsons Echo, November 28, 1938. Seven seniors of the 1938 Parsons High School "Parsons Panthers:" *Top row left to right,* Mont Wratchford, Elwood Riley, Arthur Barr, Neil Ball; *bottom row left to right,* James Parsons, Virgil Barr, Carlton Bennett, Odford Gray, Manager, and Coach Myrl Kepner.

Hattie Virginia (Oaster) Parsons and son,
James M. Parsons

Hattie Virginia (Oaster) Parsons
James Marshall Parsons

Mary Genevia (Parsons) Gordon

Mary (Parsons) Gordon and nephew James M. Parsons

Mary Genevia (Parsons) Gordon

Left to right Mary (Parsons) Gordon, unknown, Margaret (Parsons) Halfin, Hattie (Oaster) Parsons, and James E. Parsons

Front left to right Carol (Gordon) Carter, Nancy (Gordon) Everson, Mary (Parsons) Gordon, Worley Parsons, Judith A. Parsons, James E. Parsons
Back left to right Kenneth L. Gordon, Hattie (Oaster) Parsons, and James M. Parsons

Kenneth Lee Gordon (1920-2005)
Mary Genevia (Parsons) Gordon (1924-)

Fiftieth Anniversary of St. George United Methodist Women. *Left to right:* Lena Sturms, Juanita, Nestor, Hattie Parsons, Jane Pifer, Mildred Pifer, Freda Parsons and Lena Jones

FORMATION OF TUCKER COUNTY

DR. SOLOMON PARSONS APPOINTED COMMISSIONER

Solomon Parsons was instrumental in the formation of Tucker County from Randolph County in 1856. Tucker County was originally part of Orange County, Virginia, that was formed from Spotsylvania County. In 1738, that vast region was divided into the districts of Augusta and Frederick, and was to be organized into counties as soon as they attained sufficient population. In July 1775, the Virginia Convention recognized the District of West Augusta, separate from Augusta. Boundaries were not established until October 1776, when, by an Act of the General Assembly of Virginia, the District of West Augusta was divided into distinct counties: Monongalia, Ohio, and Yohogania. (Fansler1-4)

Morgantown is the county seat of Monongalia County. Harrison County was formed from Monongalia in 1784, with Clarksburg as the county seat. Randolph County was created from part of Harrison County in 1787, and Beverly was allotted the county seat. Tucker County was formed from Randolph County in 1856, after being part of Randolph for sixty-nine years. (Fansler 4)

Traveling to the county seat of Beverly for court and county business promoted a hardship for those living in the northern part of Randolph County. There was much discussion of forming a new county and significant steps were taken the winter of 1854-1855. A public meeting was held at the residence of Enoch Minear in present-day St. George; and a petition was produced bearing numerous signatures, which was sent immediately to the Assembly at Richmond. (Fansler 4)

Albert G. Reger of Upshur County was state senator, and Squire Bosworth of Randolph County was the delegate in the Virginia

General Assembly. Bosworth was a reputed apathetic representative and speaker who remained silent during most of the time that the subject of a new county was discussed. Reger, on the other hand, was absent from the Assembly due to illness, during the time that the bill for the new county was before the Assembly. (Fansler 4-5) William Ewin, a prominent and determined attorney of St. George, was sent to Richmond to lobby for the new county, hopefully assuring its success. (Fansler 5)

A member of the Assembly from Lewis County, Judge John Brannon, was a prominent and respected statesman with the ability to exert much influence. He sponsored the new county and made the motions to bring the bill before the Assembly. Judge Brannon also made the motion in the Virginia Assembly that the new county be named Tucker, for Henry Saint George Tucker Sr. and that the county seat be named Saint George, in honor of his son, Henry Saint George Tucker Jr. (Fansler 5, 10-11)

The Virginia General Assembly passed an Act forming Tucker County on Friday, March 7, 1856. The assembly further appointed five commissioners, William Ewin, Jacob W. See, William Rust Parsons, Arnold Bonnifield and Solomon Parsons to organize the new county. (Fansler 219)

On Monday, March 24, 1856, these men met in St. George. This was the first of many meetings that would divide Tucker County into three magisterial districts, establish a voting place within each district, and appoint one conductor and five commissioners to supervise an election to be held on May 22, 1856. (Fansler 219)

ACT FORMING TUCKER COUNTY

"Chap. 110 –An ACT to form the county of Tucker out of a part of Randolph county.

Passed March 7, 1856

1.   Be it enacted by the general assembly, that so much of the county o Randolph as is contained within the following boundary lines, to wit Beginning at Fairfax's corner stone, and running thence with the division line between Hardy and Randolph counties, to the corner of Pendleton county; thence with a straight line to the fork of Red Creek; thence down Red Creek to its mouth on the Dry Fork of Cheat River; thence by straight line to the point where the Pheasant Run road crosses Laurel Hill; thence with the top of Laurel Hill to the Barbour county line; thenc with said Barbour county line to the corner of Preston county, and with the line of Preston county to the beginning – shall form one distinct an new county, and shall be called and known by the name of The Count of Tucker: provided, that no part of the county of Preston shall hereafte be annexed to said county of Tucker without the consent of a majority o the voters of Preston county, ascertained at some general election.

2.   The court-house or seat of justice of said county of Tucker shall b located on the lands of Enoch Minear on the east side of Cheat River and near the mouth of Mill run; which said seat of justice shall be know as Saint George.

3.   The following persons (William Ewin, Jacob W. Lee, Solomon Parsons William R. Parsons and Arnold Bonnifield) shall be and are hereb appointed commissioners, a majority of whom may act, for the purpos of selecting the site for a court-house, jail and other public buildings fo said county of Tucker; who are hereby required to meet at the house o Enoch Minear on the fourth Monday in March next ensuing the passag of this act, or within thirty days from and after that day: and within te days after their meeting, ascertain and determine at what point or plac on the lands of the said Enoch Minear, in the said county, it is the mos suitable and proper to erect a court-house, and such other necessar buildings and fixtures as the convenience of the county requires, unde the existing laws, for holding courts and conducting business incider thereto; and shall lay off, in the most convenient form, a lot or lots o land for that purpose, not exceeding in quantity two acres; and sha ascertain the value thereof. Whereupon the said commissioners, or majority of them acting in this behalf, shall make their report in writin to the county court of Tucker, when organized, the manner in which the

shall have executed the duties required of them by this act, and of their proceedings in relation thereto, designating the point or place agreed upon, the value of the lot or lots of land, and name or names of the owners thereof. And the place so ascertained and determined upon by the said commissioners, or a majority of them, shall be deemed and taken as the permanent place for holding the courts of Tucker, now required by law to be holden for the several counties of this commonwealth. And the court for the county of Tucker shall thereupon provide for the payment of the valuation of said lot or lots of land so ascertained, in the manner now required by law, where lands shall not be already provided and appropriated for that purpose.

4.   The commissioners aforesaid shall also lay off the said county of Tucker into three magisterial districts, select points at which elections shall be holden in each district, and appoint a conductor and five commissioners (any three of whom may act) to superintend the elections to be holden for said county of Tucker, on the fourth Thursday in May next.

5.   It shall be the duty of all persons residing within the limits of the said county of Tucker, who are not entitled to vote for members of the general assembly, to attend at the respective election precincts so selected by the commissioners aforesaid, on the fourth Thursday of May in the year eighteen hundred and fifty-six, elect a sheriff, a clerk of the county court, a clerk of the circuit court, a commissioner of the revenue, overseers of the poor, commonwealth's attorney, and a surveyor for the said county of Tucker; and the voters residing in the magisterial district shall elect for that district four justices of the peace, and one constable. The election of the justices of the peace shall be certified to the governor of the commonwealth by the several conductors and commissioners superintending and conducting said elections, who, after they shall be commissioned and qualified according to law, shall meet at the house of Enoch Minear on the fourth Monday in the next month after that in which they shall be so commissioned; and a majority of them being present, shall fix upon a place in the said county of Tucker for holding the courts of the said county, until the necessary buildings shall be constructed on the site designated by the commissioners aforesaid.

6.   The said justices shall, at the first term of the county court of said county, choose one of their own body, who shall be presiding justice of the county court, and whose duty it shall be to attend each term of said court.

7.   The commissioners and conductors of the elections aforesaid shall certify to the said county court of Tucker, at its first term, or at some

subsequent term, as soon as practicable, the election of the said clerks of the county and circuit courts, commonwealth's attorney, surveyor, and commissioner of the revenue, who shall, after having given bonds and security, and being qualified according to the law, enter upon the discharge of the duties of their offices respectively.

8. The commissioners herein before appointed to lay off the county of Tucker into magisterial districts shall be allowed each a compensation of two dollars per day for their services aforesaid.

9. The term of office of the commissioner of the revenue of the said county of Tucker shall commence on the first day of February eighteen hundred and fifty-seven; and the commissioner of the revenue for the said county of Randolph is hereby required to discharge the duties of his office in the limits of the said new county of Tucker for the present year; and he is hereby directed to keep the list taken by him in the said county of Tucker separate and distinct from the list of said county of Randolph, and make return of the same in the manner now prescribed by law, in the same manner as if appointed commissioner of the revenue for the said county of Tucker.

10. The treasurer of the school commissioners of the county of Randolph shall be and is hereby required to pay to the treasurer of the school commissioners of the new county of Tucker, upon the order of the commissioners last mentioned, out of the fixed and surplus quotas of the school fund of the said county of Randolph for the present year (eighteen hundred and fifty-six,) such sum as shall seem to them to be in due proportion to the population of the said new county of Tucker, taken from the said county of Randolph, including any balance now remaining unexpended; as also of the due proportion as aforesaid, accruing from said quotas to which Randolph county is or may be entitled for any former year. And it shall be the duty of the second auditor to reapportion the fixed and surplus school quota of the county of Randolph for the next fiscal year, and subsequent years, between the said county of Randolph and the new county of Tucker, agreeably to their respective number of white tithables, which may be returned therein by the commissioners of the revenue for the present year eighteen hundred and fifty-six.

11. It shall be lawful for the sheriff of the county of Randolph to collect and make distress for any public dues or officers' fees which may remain unpaid by the inhabitants of the said county of Tucker at the time when this act shall commence and be in force; and shall be accountable for the same in line manner as if this act had never been passed.

12. The court of the county of Randolph shall retain jurisdiction of all actions and suits pending before them on the fifteenth day of June next, and shall try and determine the same, and award execution thereon, except cases wherein both parties reside within the next county; which, together with the papers, shall, after that day, be removed to the court of the county of Tucker, and there be tried and determined.

13. The said county of Tucker shall be in and attached to the twenty-first judicial circuit, and the circuit court thereof shall be holden on the eighth day of March and eighth day of August in every year, and be the same brigade district with the county of Randolph.

14. The county of Tucker shall belong to the same congressional district, the same senatorial district, and the same electoral district (for choosing electors for president and vice president of the United States) with the county of Randolph, and shall vote with the county of Randolph for a member of the house of delegates.

15. The county courts of the said county shall be holden on the second Monday in each month, and the quarterly sessions of the said county of Tucker shall be holden in the months of March, June, August and November in each year.

16. The surveyor hereafter elected for the county of Tucker, in the mode prescribed by law, together with the surveyor of the county of Randolph, shall run and mark the lines between the said county of Tucker and the county of Randolph, (from which it is formed,) agreeably and in conformity with the provisions of the seventh sections of the forty-seventh chapter of the Code of Virginia.

17. The commissioners appointed by this act to designate and fix upon the site for the public buildings in the said county, and to lay off and district said county, shall be allowed and paid the sum of two dollars for every day they shall actually be engaged in the duties aforesaid; to be provided for and paid out of the county levy of the said county of Tucker.

18. The first county court for the said county of Tucker shall be holden on the second Monday in July next.

19. This act shall be in force from its passage."
    (Fansler 5-9) (Number 3 should read Jacob W. See)

TUCKER COUNTY ELECTIONS

The three Magisterial Districts ultimately established wer Hannahsville, St. George, and Black Fork. Adam H. Bowman' residence in Hannahsville served as the voting place for that distric Enoch Minear's residence in St. George served the St. Georg District, and the voting place in Black Fork District was th residence of Andrew Fansler in Hendricks. (Fansler 219)

In 1856, there were no parties, nominations, or printed ballots There was no Republican Party until after the Civil War began Candidates were either Democrats or Whigs and simply announce that he was a candidate and solicited the votes. The ballots were a write-ins. (Fansler 219, 221)

The first Tucker County election was held on Thursday, May 22 1856, and the results for the county offices were as follows: Sheriff Jesse Parsons; County Clerk, Arnold Bonnifield; Circuit Clerk Arnold Bonnifield; Prosecuting Attorney, Rufus Maxwell; Assessor Daniel C. Adams and Surveyor, Solomon Bonner. District officer elected in each district were four justices of the peace, one constable one overseer of the poor, and they were elected as follows Hannahsville District: Justice of the Peace, Adam H. Bowman James W. Miller, John Jones and Jacob Dumire; Constable, James A Goff and Overseer of the Poor, Daniel K. Dumire. St. Georg District: Justice of the Peace, John Kalar, Israel Phillips, Francis D Talbott and John Yokum; Constable, Alfred Phillips and Overseer o the Poor, Jonathan M. Parsons. Black Fork District as follows Justice of the Peace, Jacob H. Long, Ebenezer Flanagan, Jacob Kala and Enos Carr; Constable, Garrett J. Long and Overseer of the Poor Abraham Parsons. (Fansler 220-221)

The terms of five of the county officers expired in 1858. In th general election on May 27, 1858, the following were elected County Clerk, Arnold Bonnifield; Circuit Clerk, William Ewin

Surveyor, David Wheeler; Sheriff, Jesse Parsons and Assessor, Daniel C. Adams. In 1860, the terms of three county offices expired, and in the general election held on May 24, 1860, the following were elected: Prosecuting Attorney, Rufus Maxwell, Sheriff, Abraham Parsons and Assessor, Daniel C. Adams. (Fansler 221-222)

There were five voting places in the county by 1860. St. George District had established two new voting places, Thomas Mason's residence and the new courthouse that had been built in 1858. Black Fork district had two others as well, Ebenezer Flanagan's residence at Flanagan Hill and Abraham Parsons' residence at Parsons. Hannahsville District continued to use Adam H. Bowman's residence. (Fansler 222)

When the Civil War came to Tucker County most of the officers were southern sympathizers. In May 1861, they raised a Confederate flag over the courthouse at St. George, which earned the disfavor of the Restored Government of Virginia. Troops were sent straight away to capture the flag and punish the offenders. They confiscated the flag but the offenders were not to be found. (Fansler 222)

The Restored Government of Virginia held seven elections in Tucker County in an attempt to establish a sympathetic county government and succeeded only with armed force. Under military guard, the first such election was held on June 29, 1861, in the residence of Adam H. Bowman at Hannahsville, to elect a delegate to represent Tucker and Randolph counties in the Legislature of the Restored Government in Wheeling. The Confederates attempted to break it up only to have Lieutenant Robert McChesney killed. About twenty votes were cast for Solomon Parsons. There was no official return made of the election, thus, Solomon Parsons was duly elected according to the demands of war. (Fansler 223)

Only two polls were open, the courthouse and Adam H. Bowman's residence, on December 14, 1861, for the second Restored Government election. All county officers were to be

elected except an assessor. Justices and a constable were to b
elected for their respective districts. Daniel C. Adams was elected t
both county and circuit clerkships. The others elected were a
follows: Moses B. Butterfield, prosecuting attorney; Andrew L
Moore, sheriff; and Solomon Bonner, surveyor. Justices of th
Peace were as follows: Jacob Dumire, David Wheeler, John White
William T. White and W.J. Gable and for Constable, George W
Adams and William Thompson for their districts. Oddly, in th
particular election a record was kept of the name of each voter an
how he voted. Sansome E. Parsons and Solomon Parsons wer
included among the twenty-one voters. (Fansler 223-224)

All the polls were open on April 3, 1862, for the third Restore
Government election with the exception of Flanagan Hill. Th
purpose of the election was to ratify a proposed new state, and
constitution for the new state; and to elect justices in Black Fork an
St. George districts, a constable in Hannahsville and an overseer c
the poor in St. George. The proposed new state and constitutio
were approved without opposition. Jacob W. Parsons, William Rus
Parsons, Jacob Flanagan and Jacob Kalar were elected Black For
justices. Fredrick Dumire and J.M.L. Porter were elected St. Georg
justices.   N.C. Graham was elected Hannahsville constable an
Adam White was elected overseer of the poor for St. George Distric
(Fansler 224)

The fourth Restored Government election took place on May 2.
1862, with polls open at Hannahsville, St. George and Horsesho
Run. The purpose of this election was to vote for a governo
lieutenant governor and attorney general of the Restore
Government and a combined county-circuit clerk, sheriff, assesso
surveyor, justices and constable. Francis Harrison Pierpoint wa
elected governor; Daniel Polsley, lieutenant governor; and James S
Wheat, attorney general. On the local level, Adam H. Bowman wa
elected county-circuit clerk; Andrew D. Moore, sheriff; William W
Parsons, assessor; and Solomon Bonner, surveyor. In Hannahsvill
District, Isaac S. James was elected constable. In the St. Georg

District, Adam Dumire was elected constable, and Joseph Neville was elected overseer of the poor. (Fansler 224)

The purpose of the fifth Restored Government election held on June 28, 1862, was to elect a justice, as David Wheeler had resigned, and to elect a constable. Robert Phillips was elected constable, without opposition, but a tie occurred for justice between A.C. Scott and Adam Dumire. The poll at the St. George courthouse was the only one open. (Fansler 225)

The sixth Restored Government election was held on March 26, 1863, with three polls open, Hannahsville, St. George, and Horseshoe Run. The purpose of this election was to ratify an amendment to the constitution of the proposed State of West Virginia. It carried in all three districts. (Fansler 225)

The seventh Restored Government election took place on May 28, 1863. Three polls were open at Hannahsville, St. George, and Pine Grove Church on Horseshoe Run. The results were: Arthur Ingraham Boreman, governor; Edgar J. Boyer, secretary of state; Campbell Tarr, treasurer; Samuel Crane, auditor; A.B. Caldwell, attorney general; and Ralph L. Berkshire, William A. Harrison, and James H. Brown, judges of the Court of Appeals. John Adams Dille, judge of the Circuit Court, was unopposed. No votes were cast for state senator, with the exception of one for David S. Minear who was not a candidate. For House of Delegates, Charles Burke received 30 votes; Cyrus Kittle and Willis J. Drummond received two votes each. Within the county, Adam H. Bowman was elected circuit-county clerk, Jacob Dumire was elected sheriff, and Moses B. Butterfield was elected prosecuting attorney. William Thompson was elected surveyor. (Fansler 225-226)

After West Virginia became a state, only four war-time elections were held in Tucker County. In the first election, held on October 22, 1863, only two county officers were voted on. William W. Parsons was elected assessor and Jacob W. Parsons was elected sheriff. (Fansler 226-227)

It required ninety-seven days to accomplish the second election, January 23 to April 28, 1864, and only the offices of treasurer and sheriff were voted on, along with the district offices. Sansome E. Parsons received the most votes, forty-five, but Adam H. Bowman was declared treasurer, who did not receive a single vote. Harrison Moore was elected sheriff. Black Fork District failed to complete its election, so the county court filled the vacancies by appointment as follows: Cornelius Parsons, clerk of township; William W. Parsons, township treasurer; Adam L. Corrick, constable; and Jacob W. Parsons, overseer of roads. (Fansler 227)

On October 27, 1864, the results were as follows: Prosecuting Attorney, Spencer Dayton; County Treasurer, Adam H. Bowman, again having received no votes over Sansome E. Parsons with eighty-six votes; County Clerk, John Jackson Adams; County Surveyor, Cornelius H. Parsons; Assessor, Daniel C. Adams with forty-two votes over William Rust Parsons who had with forty-five votes. In two separate elections, Sansome E. Parsons was unable to displace Adam H. Bowman who had not received a single vote; both were strong Union men. (Fansler 227-228, 229)

In the October 1864, election for prosecuting attorney, Spencer Dayton tied with J.C.A. Brown, thirty-three votes each. Yet, Dayton was certified for the office by the county court. In the same election, Daniel C. Adams was certified as assessor with three votes less than William Rust Parsons. Adams was a Union man, while Parsons was a southern sympathizer and slave owner. (Fansler 229-230)

During the general election of October 25, 1866, Arnold Bonnifield defeated Sansome E. Parsons for treasurer by a vote of 135 to 23. A confirmed Confederate Rebel, Bonnifield was unable to take the "test oath," therefore could not qualify. An established unionist, Sansome E. Parsons was appointed interim treasurer by the county court on June 21, 1867. (Fansler 230)

On October 24, 1867, a special election was held to elect members of the legislature, a county superintendent of schools and to fill the term of Sansome E. Parsons. Jacob Dumire was elected treasurer over Andrew Pifer by a vote of twenty to five. (Fansler 230)

Obviously corruption took place during the elections held for the period of the Civil War. Manipulation is defined by the mere act of holding five elections within the period of one year. Few candidates, during and after the war, could conscientiously take the "test oath," which was required by law. It was engineered to prevent those with southern sympathies from holding public offices.

TEST OATH

"I do solemnly swear that I will support the Constitution of the United States and of this State; that I have never voluntarily borne arms against the United States; that I have voluntarily given no aid or comfort to persons engaged in armed hostility thereto, by countenancing, counseling, or encouraging them in the same; that I have not sought, accepted or attempted to exercise the functions of any office whatever, under any authority in hostility to the United States; that I have not yielded a voluntary support to any pretended Government, Authority, Power, or Constitution within the United States, hostile or inimical thereto; and that I take this obligation freely, without mental reservation or purpose of evasion."
(Fansler 229)

FIRST COUNTY OFFICIALS

A record follows of the first Parsonses that served Tucker County in an official role.

Treasurer
Sansome Elliott Parsons, Term 1867-1868
(Fansler 231)

Assessor of Tucker County
William W. Parsons (Republican), Term 1862-1865
(Fansler 232)

Prosecuting Attorney of Tucker County
Adonijah B. Parsons, (Democrat), Term 1877-1881
(Fansler 235)

Sheriff of Tucker County
Jesse Parsons, (Democrat), Term 1856-1858, 1858-1860
(Fansler 236)

Abraham Parsons, (Democrat), Term 1860-1861
(Fansler 236)

Jacob Ward Parsons, (Republican), Term 1863-1867
(Fansler 236)

Ward Parsons, (Democrat), Term 1877-1881
(Fansler 236)

Surveyor of Tucker County
Cornelius H. Parsons, (Democrat), Term 1865-1866
(Fansler 237)

Joseph Parsons, (Democrat), Term 1867-1869, 1869-1871
(Fansler 238)

Adonijah B. Parsons, (Democrat), Term 1871-1873
(Fansler 238)

Members of the House of Delegates Representing Tucker County
Solomon Parsons, (Republican), Term 1861-1863 (To the Restored Government of Virginia at Wheeling, (West) Virginia.
(Fansler 239)

Adonijah B. Parsons, (Democrat) Term 1883-1885
(Fansler 240)

Commissioners of Tucker County
Solomon Parsons and William Rust Parsons, Term 1856-1856, appointed by an Act of the Virginia General Assembly March 7, 1856, for the sole purpose of organizing the county. After the first election on May 22, 1856, their appointment as commissioners automatically terminated. (Fansler 242)

William Rust Parsons and Jacob Ward Parsons, Term 1860-1861
(Fansler 242)

Jacob Ward Parsons and William Rust Parsons, Term 1861-1862
(Fansler, pp. 242-243)

Sansome E. Parsons and Jacob Ward Parsons, Term 1862-1863
(Fansler 243)

Job Parsons, Jr., Term 1866-1867, 1867-1868, 1868-1869, 1869-1870, 1870-1871 (Fansler 243)

Sansome E. Parsons, Term 1877-1881, 1887-1889, 1889-1891, 1891-1893 (Fansler 243- 244) Sansome E. Parsons resigned April 7, 1892.

James Parsons, Term 1889-1891, 1891-1893, 1893-1895
(James Parsons died between January 3 and April 3, 1893)
(Fansler 244)

TUCKER COUNTY COURTHOUSE WAR

Tucker County's first courthouse was the Ann Eliza Church in St. George near the mouth of Mill Run. It was leased from the trustees as a temporary courthouse from 1856 to 1859. (Fansler 247)

The second courthouse was built in 1858 by Samuel W. Bowman for $5,000. It was a brick building erected on the site were Fort Minear had been built in 1776. The court was petitioned on February 11, 1858, to erect the courthouse on the Isaac Parsons farm in Holly Meadows, but this could not be done as the original Act directed the courthouse be located in St. George on the land of Enoch Minear. The bricks were molded and baked on the south side of Mill Run. David Ridenour of Aurora made and laid the brick, and Daniel K. Dumire furnished the lumber and cut it on his up-and-down sawmill on Mill Run. This was the courthouse from 1859 to 1893.
(Fansler 247-248)

The largest bell in Tucker County graced the new courthouse in St. George. It was donated by one of St. George's most prominent citizens, William Ewin. The bell was cast by the Baltimore Bell Works in 1859, shipped to Rowlesburg by railway, and hauled by wagon to St. George. The Ewin bell was used on Sundays, to call people to worship. It rang the alarm for fires, announced a death, and called the court into session. During the Civil War, it alerted the citizens, "IMBODEN is coming! (Fansler 248)

The year of 1888, changed the course of history for St. George. A devastating fire occurred that destroyed three flourishing hotels. It was during this time that the railway by-passed the town. The new town of Parsons sprang up near the convergence of the Shavers Fork and Black Fork rivers. Parsons was incorporated on June 12, 1893, and in just five years, it was larger than St. George. But the citizens of Parsons were pushing for the county seat to be moved long before Parsons was incorporated. (Fansler 248- 249)

On February 12, 1889, Ward Parsons and a number of cohorts filed a petition with the county court, requesting a popular vote on relocating the county seat. The court dismissed this petition as being out of order. (Fansler 249)

On April 9, 1890, Ward Parsons and 205 followers filed the second petition with the court. Sansome E. Parsons of St. George District, James Parsons of Fairfax District, and James Henry Lambert of Dry Fork District formed the county court. They ordered a vote to be taken at the next general election on November 4, 1890. (Fansler 249)

Ward Parsons filed two more petitions with the county court, on July 11, 1890, and October 8, 1890, prior to the general election. The court's only recourse was to table these petitions. By law, a vote of three-fifths of the majority was required to remove the county seat from St. George. The vote failed in the general election with 689 in favor and 576 against. (Fansler 249)

On January 6, 1892, Ward Parsons, Job Parsons Jr. and close to 700 others filed 7 petitions with the county court requesting relocation. The court ordered another vote to be taken on the next general election day, November 8, 1892. The court was then composed of Sansome E. Parsons, James Parsons and Michael Myers. The vote in this election was 820 for relocation and 569 against, lacking 14 votes of being three-fifths majority. (Fansler 249)

Determined to have the courthouse moved, on January 4, 1893, Ward Parsons and 669 others filed seven more petitions with the county court requesting another vote on relocation. This court of James Parsons, Michael Myers and James W. Campbell were exhausted with the repeated petitions. They ordered a special election to be held on April 28, 1893. (Fansler 250)

Finally, on April 28, 1893, the vote for relocation carried, 1,110 for relocation and 514 against. The supporters had their required three-fifths majority. The court ordered the county seat to be moved from St. George to Parsons on Monday, August 7, 1893. (Fansler 250)

On July 21, 1893, Ward Parsons, Sansome E. Parsons, C. J. McKinney, William N. Doolittle, J. M. Talbott, John W. Pifer, C. E. Glenn, and Lemuel W. Parsons offered a building for a temporary courthouse, rent-free for four years, ending on August 7, 1897. This building was located on Main Street. A contract was awarded to the Poling Brothers for the removal of the county's property, records, safes and furniture. They were directed to move the property from St. George to the temporary courthouse at Parsons for the sum of $120. (Fansler 251-252)

An ex-sheriff, Adam C. Minear, and the County Clerk, William M. Cayton, continued to fight the relocation of the county seat. They went to Charleston in July 1893 to secure an injunction. When it was learned in Parsons that a move was underway to stop the relocation, Ward Parsons and others gathered and decided that they would go to St. George at night and seize the county records. (Fansler 252-253)

On August 1, 1893, nearly two hundred men gathered in Parsons, under the direction of Ward Parsons. With pistols and clubs in hand, they set out for St. George in wagons, buggies, and on saddle horses, or by foot. They traveled eight miles of narrow roads and forded Cheat River three times. (Fansler 253)

News of the invasion had reached the people of St. George, and they had prepared themselves with guns, clubs, and stones. They gathered along the street fronting the courthouse, and when the Parsons crowd arrived in St. George about 9:30 p.m., Sheriff Will E. Cupp immediately ordered the crowd to disperse. (Fansler 254)

When the news came down that the Parsons crowd was coming, the courthouse was locked and barred, but the invaders broke the windows and opened the doors from within. They loaded the county's records and equipment, including the Ewin bell, onto their wagons and set off for Parsons. Some shots had been fired throughout the affair, mostly to create fear, but fortunately no one was injured. St. George was apparently overwhelmed by the numbers of the opposition and made little move to interfere. (Fansler 254)

At daylight, on Wednesday, August 2, 1893, the raiders reached Parsons. A temporary courthouse was set up in a nearly-completed store building on Main Street. This served as the courthouse from 1893 to 1900, the time it took to erect a new courthouse. This building presently serves the McClain Printing Company as a warehouse. (Fansler 255)

Parsons became the county seat of Tucker County, by law, August 7, 1893, although the records had been unlawfully removed from St. George five days previous to that date. (Fansler 372) Apparently the citizens of Parsons preferred a clock in the new courthouse as opposed to the Ewin Bell. Amer Lake, father of banker Hubert Bascom Lake, purchased the bell and donated it to the First United Methodist Church of Parsons that was built in 1892. (Fansler 257)

156

The Intelligencer of Wheeling, West Virginia, covered the event a
follows:

COUNTY SEAT WAR

Down in Tucker County Has An Unique Ending

RECORDS MOVED IN NIGHT TIME

By a Crowd of Three Hundred Self-Constituted Officials-Citizens of S
George Armed with Rifles, but Overawed by Superior Numbers-The Cou
Had Set August 7 for the Removal, but the "Boys" Took Matters Out of th
Hands of the Authorities and Will Now be Prosecuted for Their Conduc
Dynamite and Gunshots Play a Part in the Drama.
Special Dispatch to the Intelligencer

Bretz, W.VA., August 3. – A very exciting incident occurred in this count
Tuesday night. Plans were arranged to forcibly remove the county records fro
the court house at St. George to Parsons, and a regiment of about three hundre
men left Parsons for the old court house for that purpose. While traveling alon
the lonely road to St. George several shots were fired at the crowd by the S
George picket guards along the path. When nearing their destination several blas
of dynamite were discharged. At St. George on several street corners small squad
of citizens were congregated, armed with rifles, but the visitors were not moleste
Upon the arrival of the Parsons and Davis crowd the sheriff notified them t
disband, but the order was disobeyed, and entrance to the building was effecte
through the windows, after which the locks were unfastened, the doors throw
open, and the crowd took possession of the contents of the building.

The men have arrived with the court records and everything of value belonging t
the county in their possession, and deposited them in the new court house a
Parsons. Several fistic disputes took place on the trip, but no one was seriousl
injured. It is reported that arrests will be made at once, as the court had set Augus
7 for removal of the records. It was a disgraceful occurrence and the best citizen
regard it as a disgrace to Tucker county. Seventy tickets were sold at Davis fo
Parsons on this occasion via West Virginia Central & Pittsburgh railroad. Th
members of the crowd of record movers acted without authority and may b
prosecuted for contempt of court. In addition the affair is likely to breed a feu
which will be serious in its results.
(Accessed on-line at wvculture.org)

BLOOD MAY FLOW
ARMED MEN GUARDING the COURT HOUSE at PARSONS

THE TUCKER COUNTY SEAT WAR
Growing Serious and the Situation is Grave

RUMORS THAT A FINAL ATTEMPT
Will be Made by St. George Citizens to Recapture the County Records Which were Removed by a Body of Parsonites Last Week- A History of the Trouble-The People Overwhelmingly Voted for Removal, The St. George People Attempt to Prevent it by Legal Means-Bloodshed may yet Result.
Special Dispatch by the Intelligencer

Bretz, W.Va., August 8. – Another chapter has been added to the Tucker county court house episode. Last night about nine o'clock word was received from St. George that a large crowd was being mustered to forcibly remove the court records from Parsons to St. George. The courthouse bell was rung for twenty minutes, ringing out the alarm that an attempt should be made to break into the temporary courthouse and remove the contents. In less than five minutes fully fifty armed men were on the scene ready for action. Work was commenced at once erecting breast works in front of the building across the street and strict orders were given by the captain to use their guns freely if necessary to prevent the destruction of the court house, county papers and private property, as Parsons is now legally the county-seat, the bid having been awarded for the removal of the records by the seventh.

Many were armed with rifles, repeaters, old army muskets, hatchets and acid. About one o'clock two successive shots were fired opposite the Parsons City Hotel, which is a half square from the courthouse, and almost instantly every armed individual was at his post in the trench back of the breastworks. It proved to be a false alarm. Up to 3 o'clock a.m., the St. George contingent had not put in their appearances. All this time some were doing picket duty while others were sleeping. At 5 nothing serious had occurred, and the guards went to breakfast.

Court is in session today at St. George but nothing can be heard. Judge Hoke of the circuit court has appointed guards at the courthouse at Parsons to protect records and public property, with the privilege of adding recruits. If the St. George people put in their appearances surely blood will be shed and many will be killed. At present everything is quiet, but trouble is expected tonight after the action of the court is known. (Accessed on-line at wvculture.org)

IF BELLS COULD TALK
Mrs. Meade Gutshall

If the power of speech could be given a bell,
I am sure that ours, great stories could tell;
But since bells cannot talk, nor stories tell,
I will give you some history of our bell.

The bell was shipped from Baltimore in 1859,
A gift from William Ewin, a citizen sublime;
The journey was rough, and the roads were bad,
But the bell arrived safely—everyone was glad.

In the St. George courthouse the bell was hung,
And placed in the tower, soon to be rung;
The dong of the bell was heard with glee,
It was the first public bell in the county, you see.

The community messenger the bell soon became,
Sad news and good news the bell did proclaim;
On Sunday it called the people to church,
To learn of God – the Scriptures to search.

At times it rang out for court, fire, and death,
Everyone soon learned, just what the bell saith;
Then one night the bell was carried away,
By some men to Parsons, there to stay.

At first it was used just for the opening of court,
And it seemed that its life was growing short;
And soon a clock was put in its place,
The old bell was doomed just to take up space.

But the life of the faithful bell did not end,
The bell was saved by a faithful friend;
Mr. Amer Lake purchased the bell,
And to a church home he brought it to dwell.

The First Methodist Church he chose for a home,
And now it still rings, calls to all who might roam;
For more than 100 years the bell has been tolling,
Just the sound of it, to all is consoling.

And tho' it is old, it still rings today,
Calling God's people to worship and pray;
May we be as faithful as the old, old bell,
And when life here is over, all will be well.
(Courtesy of Barbara Gutshall Roy)

DELEGATE SOLOMON PARSONS

The American Civil War was a military conflict between the United States of America (Union) and the Confederate States of America (Confederacy) that began in 1861 and ended in 1865. The chief cause of the Civil War was slavery. The southern states, including the eleven states that formed the Confederacy, depended on slavery to support their economy. Southerners used slave labor to produce crops, especially cotton. Although slavery was illegal in the Northern states, only a small proportion of the Northerners actively opposed it. The main debate between the North and the South on the eve of the war was whether slavery should be permitted in the Western territories, recently acquired during the Mexican War, including New Mexico, part of California and Utah. Opponents of slavery were concerned about its expansion, in part, because they did not want to compete against slave labor.

By 1860, the North and South had developed into two very different regions. Different social, economic, and political points of view dating from colonial times gradually drove the two sections farther and farther apart. Each tried to impose its point of view on the country as a whole. Although compromises had kept the Union together for many years, in 1860 the situation was volatile. Abraham Lincoln's election was viewed by the South as a threat to slavery and ignited the war.

The Civil War began on April 12, 1861, when Confederate General P. G. T. Beauregard opened fire on Fort Sumter in Charleston Harbor, South Carolina. The war ended on May 26, 1865, when the last Confederate army surrendered. The war took more than 600,000 lives and destroyed property valued at $5 billion. The war brought freedom to four million black slaves, and it opened wounds that have not yet completely healed over 140 years later.

As soon as it was certain that Lincoln had won, the South Carolina legislature summoned a special convention. It met on December 17, 1860, in Charleston. Three days later the convention unanimously passed an ordinance dissolving "the union now subsisting between South Carolina and other States." Similar conventions were held by other Southern states, and similar ordinances were adopted, although not by unanimous votes.

In April, Lincoln called for states to send militias for national service to suppress the rebellion. The upper South refused to send their militias to coerce the seceded states. Instead, they joined the lower South in secession, beginning with Virginia.

TIMELINE FOR WEST VIRGINIA STATEHOOD

Solomon Parsons, Delegate
James W. Parsons (Solomon's son), Delegate

April 17, 1861, State of Virginia Secedes

April 22, 1861, Clarksburg Convention

May 13-15, 1861, First Wheeling Convention for Statehood: No Tucker or Randolph County Representation (to consider the advisability of seceding from the seceding state of Virginia)

June 11-25, 1861, Second Wheeling Convention (First Session): Solomon Parsons and Samuel Crane, Delegates from Tucker and Randolph County

July 1-26, 1861, Reorganized Government – General Assembly: Solomon Parsons Delegate from Tucker County

August 6-21, 1861, Second Wheeling Convention for Statehood (Second Session): Solomon Parsons Delegate from Tucker County

November 26, 1861, to February 18, 1862, Constitutional Convention: James W. Parsons Delegate from Tucker County

April 3, 1862, Constitution approved for the new State of West Virginia

December 31, 1862, President Abraham Lincoln passes West Virginia Statehood Bill on the eve of the passage of the Emancipation Proclamation

June 20, 1863, West Virginia becomes the 35th state in the United States of America

WEST VIRGINIA STATEHOOD

From the earliest communities, sectionalism existed betwee western and eastern Virginia.   In 1776, the Virginia Stat Constitution granted voting rights only to white males owning a least twenty-five acres of improved or fifty acres of unimprove land. This discriminated against the small landowners in wester Virginia since many western Virginians did not own the land o which they lived.   Furthermore, regardless of population, th constitution delegated a disproportionate representation in the stat General Assembly to eastern Virginia, by allowing only tw delegates per county. (http://www.wvculture.org/history/statehoo.html)

Some time later, the Virginia General Assembly passed a numbe of acts for the benefit of western Virginia. Until now, representatio in the Senate was based upon total population, including slaves This favored eastern Virginia, which had the greater slav population.   Reapportionment of the Senate, based upon whit population, improved western Virginia's representation.   Th creation of a Board of Public Works offered hope for developin more roads and canals. State banks were finally established i western   Virginia,   at   Wheeling   and   Wincheste
(http://www.wvculture.org/history/statehoo.html)

On October 5, 1829, a convention was held in Richmond t develop a new constitution. Among several reforms, two significar issues were addressed by this constitution: Granting the vote to a white men, regardless if they owned land, and the election of th governor and judges by the people. But eastern Virginia conservatives defeated every major reform.
(http://www.wvculture.org/history/statehoo.html)

The new constitution was approved statewide by a vote of 26,05 to 15,566, even though rejected by voters in western Virginia 8,36 to 1,383.   Immediately, calls for secession began. The Genera

Assembly eased some of the sectional tension, over the next twenty years. Nineteen new western counties were organized, which provided even greater representation. Also, internal improvements were made that included the Staunton-Parkersburg Turnpike and Northwestern Turnpike. (http://www.wvculture.org/history/statehoo.html)

The issue of slavery surfaced following Nat Turner's raid in August 1831, which killed sixty-one whites in Southampton County, Virginia, and William Lloyd Garrison printed his newspaper, *The Liberator*, which marked the beginning of abolitionism. There were those who disapproved of slavery on a moral issue, and others, supported abolitionism as they felt slaves performed jobs that white laborers should be paid to do. (http://www.wvculture.org/history/statehoo.html)

In 1850, Virginia delegates gathered once more in Richmond to work on issues between eastern and western Virginia. One major issue was resolved: All white males over the age of twenty-one were granted the right to vote regardless of weather they owned property. The convention also approved the election of the governor and judges by the people. Delegates agreed to a provision that taxed property at its total value, although slaves would be valued at rates well below their actual worth. Up until this time, many eastern slaveholders paid less in property taxes, which placed a greater burden on the western counties. Efforts between the two fractions of eastern and western Virginia collapsed with the advent of the Civil War in November 1860. (http://www.wvculture.org/history/statehoo.html)

VIRGINIA SECEDES

On November 6, 1860, Abraham Lincoln was elected the 16th President of the United States, an event that outraged the southern states. The Republican Party had run on an anti-slavery platform, and many southerners felt there was no longer a place for them in the Union.

By February 1, 1861, seven states had separated from the Union. South Carolina, Mississippi, Florida, Alabama, Georgia, Louisiana, and Texas. The seceded states created the Confederate States of America and elected Jefferson Davis, a Mississippi senator, as their provisional president.

Governor John Letcher called the Virginia General Assembly into extra session on January 7, 1861. The Assembly called for a state convention to be held in Richmond on February 13. The delegates, 152 in all, met to determine Virginia's course in the immediate crisis. The newly-elected president of the convention, John Janney of Loudoun County, addressed his fellow delegates, "It is our duty on an occasion like this to elevate ourselves into an atmosphere, in which party passion and prejudice cannot exist - to conduct all our deliberations with calmness and wisdom, and to maintain, with inflexible firmness, whatever position we may find it necessary to assume." (http://www.wvculture.org/history/statehoo.html)

As the proceedings began, the general mood in the convention was against secession. On April 12, 1861, Fort Sumter surrendered to Confederate forces and three days later, President Lincoln issued a call for 75,000 troops to put down the rebellion. This convinced the majority of delegates that the time had come for Virginia to leave the Union. On April 17, 1861, delegates passed an Ordinance of Secession by a vote of 88 to 55. Led by John Carlile, western delegates withdrew from the convention, vowing to form a state government loyal to the Union. (http://www.wvculture.org/history/statehoo.html)

CLARKSBURG CONVENTION

Immediately following the secession of Virginia, a mass meeting of special interest was held in Clarksburg at the Harrison County Courthouse on April 22, 1861. Well over 1,000 citizens attended this gathering. The following preamble and resolutions were adopted without one dissenting voice.

PREAMBLE

"Whereas, the convention now in session in this State, called by the Legislature . . . has, contrary to the expectation of a large majority of the people of this State, adopted an ordinance withdrawing Virginia from the Federal Union.

And Whereas, By the law calling said Convention, it is expressly declared that no such ordinance shall have force or effect, or be of binding obligation upon the people of this State, until the same shall be ratified by the voters at the polls.

And Whereas, We have seen with regret that demonstrations of hostility, unauthorized by law, and inconsistent with the duty of law-abiding citizens, still owing allegiance to the Federal Government, have been made by a portion of the people of this State against the said Government.

And Whereas, the Governor of this Commonwealth has, by proclamation, undertaken to decide for the People of Virginia, that which they have reserved to themselves, the right to decide by their votes at the polls, and has called upon the volunteer soldiery of this State to report to him and hold themselves in readiness to make war upon the Federal Government, which Government is Virginia's Government, and must in law and of right continue so to be, until the people of Virginia shall, by their votes, and through the ballot-box that great conservator of a free people's liberties, decide otherwise.

And Whereas, The peculiar situation of Northwestern Virginia separated as it is by natural barriers from the rest of the State precludes all hope of timely succor in the hour of danger from other portions of the State, and demands that we should look to and provide for their own safety in the fearful emergency in which we now find ourselves placed by the action of our State authorities, who have disregarded the great fundamental principle upon which our beautiful system of Government is based, to wit: 'That all governmental power is derived from the consent of the governed, and have without consulting the people, placed this State in hostility to the Federal Government by seizing upon its ships and obstructing the channel at the mouth of Elizabeth river; by wresting from the Federal officers at Norfolk and Richmond the custom houses; by tearing from the Nation's property the Nation's flag, and putting in its place a bunting, the emblem of rebellion, and by marching upon the National Armory at Harper's Ferry; thus inaugurating a war without consulting those in whose name they profess to act.

And Whereas, The exposed condition of Northwestern Virginia requires that her people should be united in action, and harmonious in purpose-there being a perfect identity of interests in times of war as well as in peace-Therefore,

Be it Resolved, That it be and is hereby recommended to the people in each and all of the counties composing Northwestern Virginia to appoint delegates, not less that five in number, of their wisest, best discreetest men, to meet in Convention on the 13th day of May next to consult and determine upon such action as the people in Northwestern Virginia should take in the present fearful emergency . . ."

John Hurley, President
(www.access.wvu.edu/class/wvhistory/documents/028.pdf)

FIRST WHEELING CONVENTION

West Virginia's statehood movement began at Washington Hall in Wheeling on May 13, 1861. This was called the First Wheeling Convention and its purpose was to organize opposition to secession and remain in the Union. William B. Zinn of Preston County was appointed temporary chairman, and George Latham of Taylor County was selected as temporary secretary. (http://www.wvculture.org/history/statehood.html)

The convention included delegates from twenty-seven of fifty western Virginia counties, therefore, did not truly represent the future state of West Virginia. Of 436 delegates attending, over one-third resided in the Northern Panhandle. Tucker County had no representation. (http://www.wvculture.org/history/statehood.html)

Immediately a debate ensued over which delegates should be permitted to participate in the Convention. General John Jay Jackson of Wood County suggested seating all northwestern Virginia, but John S. Carlile insisted that only those who had been legitimately appointed by their constituencies be allowed to participate. Chester D. Hubbard of Ohio County ended the debate by proposing the creation of a committee on representation and permanent organization. (http://www.wvculture.org/history/statehood.html)

General John Jay Jackson, Waitman Willey, and most of the other delegates, argued that preemptive action against the Ordinance of Secession before it was ratified was unwise. The Ordinance had not yet been presented to the citizens of Virginia for a vote, and would not until May 23. Others, including John Carlile, sought immediate action. "Let us act, let us repudiate these monstrous usurpations; let us show our loyalty to Virginia and the Union; and let us maintain ourselves in the Union at every hazard. It is useless to cry peace when there is no peace; and I for one will repeat what was said by one of Virginia's noblest sons and greatest statesmen, 'Give me liberty or give me death!' "   (http://www.wvculture.org/history/statehood.html)

On May 14, John Carlile proposed a resolution for the creation of the new state of New Virginia.   The motion was condemned as revolutionary, and most of the Convention instead supported resolutions offered by the Committee on State and Federal Resolutions, which recommended that western Virginians elect delegates to a Second Wheeling Convention to begin on June 11, 1861, if the people of Virginia approved the Ordinance of Secession. (http://www.wvculture.org/history/statehood.html)

In an election held on May 23, 1861, the Virginia Ordinance of Secession was ratified by a vote of the people. The fifty counties of western Virginia cast 44,000 votes; of those votes, 40,000 rejected the Ordinance.   When John Letcher, the new Governor of Virginia, heard of the Wheeling convention, he issued orders stating: "Arrest, forthwith, all and every person who participated in or supported that Wheeling convention; take them dead or alive and send them to Richmond, where we will bury the dead and hang the living." (Fansler 130)

SECOND WHEELING CONVENTION

FIRST SESSION

With the approval of Virginia's Ordinance of Secession on May 23, the Second Wheeling Convention met on June 11, 1861. The meeting was held in Washington Hall and later the Custom House. The first measure adopted at the Convention ruled that eighty-eight delegates representing thirty-two counties were entitled to seats in the convention; other delegates were added later. Dr. Solomon Parsons and Samuel Crane represented Tucker and Randolph counties respectively.
http://www.wvculture.org/history/statehood.html)

President Arthur I. Boreman addressed the gathering: "In this Convention we have no ordinary political gathering. We have no ordinary task before us. We come here to carry out and execute, and it may be, to institute a government for ourselves. We are determined to live under a State Government in the United States of America and under the Constitution of the United States. It requires stout hearts to execute this purpose; it requires men of courage – of unfaltering determination; and I believe, in the gentlemen who compose this Convention, we have the stout hearts and the men who are determined in this purpose."
(http://www.wvculture.org/history/statehood.html)

On June 13, John Carlile, introduced to the Convention "A Declaration of the People of Virginia," a document calling for the reorganization of the state government on the grounds that Virginia's secession had in effect vacated all offices of the existing government. Carlile presented an ordinance for this purpose the next day, and the debate began. (http://www.wvculture.org/history/statehood.html)

Several delegates at the Convention recognized the disparity between eastern and western Virginia as conflicting and supported some sort of separation. The disagreement was over how to proceed with a separation. Dennis Dorsey of Monongalia County called for permanent separation from eastern Virginia. Carlile, however, though he had called for a similar plan during the First Wheeling Convention, persuaded the delegates that Constitutional restrictions made it necessary for the formation of a loyal government of Virginia, whose legislature could then give permission for the creation of a new state. Carlile acknowledged, "I find that even I, who first started the little stone down the mountain, have now to apply the rubbers to other gentlemen who have outrun me in the race, to check their impetuosity." On June 19, delegates of the convention unanimously supported the ordinance reorganizing the government of Virginia. (http://www.wvculture.org/history/statehood.html)

On the following day, June 20, officials were selected to fill the offices of the Restored Government of Virginia. Francis Pierpont of Marion County was elected governor, and Daniel Polsley, lieutenant governor. James Wheat of Wheeling was elected attorney general on June 21. (http://www.wvculture.org/history/statehood.html)

Dr. Solomon Parsons attended each meeting of the First Session of the Second Wheeling Convention with one exception, June 17, as Mr. Hooton of Preston County confirmed, "...he deemed it due to the Convention as well as to Dr. Parsons, of Tucker, (now absent) to state that the reason of his absence was that he was confined to his room by indisposition, but that he was now much better and would be in his seat in a few days." (http://www.wvculture.org/history/statehood.html) On June 25, 1861, the convention adjourned until August 6.

REORGANIZED GOVERNMENT
GENERAL ASSEMBLY OF VIRGINIA

Extra Session

The legislature of the General Assembly of the Reorganized Government of Virginia convened in Wheeling on July 1, 1861, in response to Governor Francis Pierpont.
(http://www.wvculture.org/history/statehood.html)

The legislative bodies consisted of persons elected to office on May 23, who remained loyal to the Union. Approximately eight senators and thirty-two delegates participated in the proceedings. The House of Delegates met in the Federal courtroom in the Custom House, while the Senate gathered at Linsly Institute. Solomon Parsons, physician and merchant, represented Tucker County.
(http://www.wvculture.org/history/statehood.html)

Daniel Frost of Jackson County was elected Speaker of the House, and newly-elected Lieutenant Governor Daniel Polsley presided over the Senate. Governor Pierpont, in an address before the legislature, disclosed that President Lincoln had pledged "...full protection..." to the people of western Virginia. The governor called on the legislature to establish "...an efficient system to protect the loyal people of the Commonwealth against the intrigues, conspiracies and hostile acts of those who adhere to our enemies."
(http://www.wvculture.org/history/statehood.html)

On July 5, Solomon Parsons was appointed to two Standing Committees: The Committee on Propositions and Grievances and the Committee on Roads and Internal Navigation.
(http://www.wvculture.org/history/statehood.html)

On July 9, the legislators elected a number of state officials, including Lucien Hagans, secretary of the commonwealth, and Campbell Tarr, treasurer. (http://www.wvculture.org/history/statehood.html)

Dr. Solomon Parsons nominated Samuel Crane of Randolph County for auditor of public accounts: "I rise for the purpose of nominating for Auditor Samuel Crane, of Randolph. My personal knowledge of Mr. Crane is such that I can truthfully recommend him. He is a self-made man, raised by his own exertions, and has probably fought his way through as much opposition as any other man in the world; and last winter in the Legislature of Virginia at Richmond, he stood up unflinchingly for the Union. While many of our bravest men quailed, Samuel Crane came out of the conflict like gold tried by fire. He is now driven from his home, for no other cause than that he is advocating the Union for which our fathers fought, and at this very moment secession forces are encamped on his farm and trampling its soil beneath their feet. If the newspaper reports can be credited the troops are now occupying the farm of Samuel Crane in Randolph County, and appropriating and destroying his property. Mr. Crane is a poor man. His all was dependant on his practice at law, with the addition of his small farm. He has been deprived of his practice, driven from his home and native county. His property has been confiscated and destroyed, and he himself dare not return. I do think, gentlemen, that Mr. Crane has claims upon the magnanimity of this body; at the same time, I feel assured that his abilities are such that he would render entire satisfaction."
(http://www.wvculture.org/history/statehood.html)

Thomas Logan of Ohio County followed with a lengthy nomination of N. Wilkinson of Wheeling. James West of Wetzel County appealed to the sympathies of the House on behalf of Mr. Crane. He was succeeded by John W. Moss of Wood County who eulogized Mr. Crane for his qualifications and strongly urged his election. The Senate was then notified of the nominations and the election ensued. Mr. Crane was declared auditor with the vote for Crane, 33, Wilkinson, 5. (http://www.wvculture.org/history/statehood.html)

The legislature proceeded to the selection of United States senators. John Carlile was unanimously elected to fill the slot of R. M. T. Hunter. Waitman T. Willey, Peter Van Winkle and Daniel Lamb were nominated to replace James M. Mason. The *Wheeling*

Intelligencer voiced its opposition to the selection of Willey, stating, "He is not, never was, nor never will be a leader. He has not the back bone for times like these . . ." Despite opposition to Willey due to his perceived conservatism, he was elected to fill the other Senate seat. On July 13, after a bitter debate, Carlile and Willey were formally seated by the United States Senate.
(http://www.wvculture.org/history/statehood.html)

On July 17, Solomon Parsons offered the following resolution that was adopted: "...that the Committee on Courts of Justice be instructed to inquire into the expediency of reporting a bill requesting the Governor to issue his proclamation requiring all citizens of the Commonwealth who have voluntarily joined the rebel army to disband within thirty days and return to their allegiance, and enacting that all who refuse to comply with the demand shall be considered aliens, their property confiscated and they compelled to leave the State." Mr. Parsons said that Bill Number 5, authorizing the organization of patrols, had lain upon the table a long time, and he was afraid it would be entirely passed by. The Rebel forces were now driven out of the country, but the Federal forces were also gone in pursuit of them. The secessionists, who had stayed at home, now that they were relieved from the wholesome fear of the Federal troops, would soon become more mischievous and dangerous than at first, unless some measures were adopted to keep them in check. This was especially the case in his own county, and indeed, in all those surrounding. Since the rout of the secession army, many of the secession troops had returned to their homes; and unless something should be done, Union men would be a worse condition than before.
(http://www.wvculture.org/history/statehood.html)

Most of the actions taken by the Legislature related to financial and military affairs of the Reorganized Government of Virginia. The extra session concluded on July 26, 1861.
(http://www.wvculture.org/history/statehood.html)

SECOND WHEELING CONVENTION

SECOND SESSION

Delegates of the Second Wheeling Convention reassemble on August 6, 1861, in the United States Court room in the Custom House in Wheeling. This convention formed a Committee on a Division of the State. After a week of deliberations, on August 13 the group formulated and presented to the convention a dismemberment ordinance. Delegates of the convention debated the boundaries of the proposed state for five days before referring the question to a committee. On August 20, the committee proposed that the newly-named state of Kanawha would consist of thirty-nine counties. But seven additional counties were to be added if the majority of voters in those counties approved: Berkeley, Greenbrier, Hampshire, Hardy, Jefferson, Morgan and Pocahontas. The committee's recommendations were adopted by a vote of fifty to twenty-eight. The proposal called for the question to be put before the voters, and if they approved, delegates chosen at the same time would assemble at Wheeling for a constitutional convention. (http://www.wvculture.org/history/statehood.html)

Solomon Parsons attended each assembly with the exception of August 7. On that day Mr. Harrison Hagans said that he was instructed by Dr. Parsons who was unwell, to have him sent for by the Sergeant-at-Arms, if any test vote should be taken. (http://www.wvculture.org/history/statehood.html)

President Arthur I. Boreman closed the convention with these remarks, "You have passed many ordinances for the purpose of carrying out the objects of your assembling, amongst them one has lately been adopted by you probably more important than any other. You have taken the initiative in the creation of a new State. This is a step of vital importance. I hope, and I pray God it may be successful; that it may not engender strife in your midst, nor bring upon us difficulties from abroad, but that its most ardent advocates may realize their fondest hopes of its complete success. . . Gentlemen, your labors have not been light; they have been arduous. You have not shrunk from the discharge of your duty, however. I feel that your constituents ought to be proud of their representatives, as I am sure that you are proud of a noble, generous and confiding constituency . . . I now hope that each and every one of you may be permitted to go to your homes and that you may find your homes, your firesides, your families, soon restored to their wanted peace and tranquility and happiness." http://www.wvculture.org/history/statehood.html)

The convention adjourned on August 21, 1861, and agreed to meet next on November 26, 1861. An election was held in 39 counties on October 24, 1861. Because it took place during a war, only 19,000 out of 48,000 eligible voters in these counties voted in this election. The voters approved the dismemberment ordinance by a vote of 18,408 to 781. The accuracy of these election results have been questioned since Union troops were stationed at many of the polls to prevent Confederate sympathizers from voting. (http://www.wvculture.org/history/statehood.html)

WEST VIRGINIA CONSTITUTIONAL CONVENTION

Following the elections held in October 1861, under th authority of "…an Ordinance to provide for the formation of a nev State out of a portion of the territory of this State," the conventioi assembled in the United States Court room in the city of Wheelin; on November 26, 1861, to create a constitution. Other issues tha were addressed included the name of the new state, boundaries, an slavery. (http://www.wvculture.org/history/statehood.html)

Solomon Parsons did not attend the Constitutional Convention Representing Tucker County in his stead was his forty-eight-year-ol son, James William Parsons, a farmer from St. George. (http://www.wvculture.org/history/statehood.html)

President John Hall appointed several standing committees o November 27. James W. Parsons was appointed to the Committee on Education, along with Gordon Battelle, William E. Stevenson Robert Hager, Thomas H. Trainer, William Walker and Georg Sheets. This committee was charged to inquire into the expediency of inserting a provision in the Constitution for the establishment of general free school system throughout the commonwealth. (http://www.wvculture.org/history/statehood.html)

On December 2, 1862, Mr. Parsons resolved that the Committee on Education inquire into the feasibility of the banks of this stat contributing from their net dividends, at least one-half of on percent, for the purposes of education. He further resolved that th Committee on Education inquire into the appropriateness of settin apart, for the purposes of education, all fines and recoveries for th use of the state, on recognizance or otherwise. (http://www.wvculture.org/history/statehood.html)

Although the voters had approved the creation of "Kanawha," many delegates opposed the name. United States Senator Waitman T. Willey drew laughter when he stated that some of his constituents found it difficult to spell. "I have no objection to any name that is convenient, though I will say that in this case I think the rose would smell sweeter by some other name," Willey commented. A lengthy debate ensued as to the best name for the new state. On December 3, after debating a great part of the day, a vote was taken: West Virginia, 30 (including the vote of James W. Parsons); Kanawha, 9; Western Virginia, 2; Allegheny, 2 and Augusta, 1. The new state was to be named West Virginia. (http://www.wvculture.org/history/statehood.html)

Determining the boundaries of the new state proved difficult for the assemblage. The Committee on Boundary proposed that an additional thirty-two counties be added to the thirty-nine already included. Debates ensued, and a number of proposed counties were rejected. Most of the counties in the Shenandoah Valley were excluded due to their control by Confederate troops and a large number of local Confederate sympathizers. Most of the eastern and southern counties did not support statehood, but were included for political, economic and military purposes. The mountain range west of the Blue Ridge became the eastern border of West Virginia to provide a defense against Confederate invasion. One of the most controversial decisions involved the Eastern Panhandle counties that supported the Confederacy. The Baltimore and Ohio Railroad ran through the Eastern Panhandle and was vital to troop movement, as well as the economy. Inclusion of these counties removed the entire railroad from the Confederacy. On December 13, the legislative body determined that the new state would include the thirty-nine original counties and five additional. Seven more counties were to be added if their voters approved.
(http://www.wvculture.org/history/statehood.html)

Slavery proved to be a controversial issue for the members of the convention. On November 30, 1861, Robert Hagar of Boone County called for a free state and proposed gradual emancipation. Delegate Gordon Battelle of Ohio County, a Methodist minister, proposed the

gradual emancipation of slaves already in the state and freedom to a children born to slaves after July 4, 1865. Although some delegate opposed Battelle's position, they knew they could not create a pro slavery document and gain approval from Congress. Following much debate and compromise, the provision written into the constitution stated, "No slave shall be brought, or free person of color be permitted to come into this State for permanent residence."
(http://www.wvculture.org/history/statehood.html)

The Committee on the Legislative Department submitted a repor on December 17, 1861, stating that the legislative power of the new state of West Virginia would be vested in a senate consisting of eighteen delegates and a house of delegates consisting of forty-six members. For the election of each, the state was to be divided into nine senatorial districts, with each district choosing two senator Every house delegate district, and the counties included within tha district, were to be entitled to at least one delegate. A heated debate ensued and continued for several days.
(http://www.wvculture.org/history/statehood.html)

Late in the day on January 9, 1862, Joseph Pomeroy of Hancoc County renewed an earlier motion to take up the second section of the legislative department report. Peter Van Winkle of Woo County moved to strike out "forty-six" and insert "fifty-four, contending that the number of delegates in the House was too smal Daniel Lamb of Ohio County and chairmen of the Legislativ Committee, believed in equal representation by delegates attained b multiplying the number of counties by two. Mr. Lamb alleged tha apportionment of delegates based on population was impossible.
(http://www.wvculture.org/history/statehood.html)

Chapman Stuart of Doddridge pleaded for thirty-six delegate: Each county would still be represented; the members would d business equally well and with only one-half the expense. Stua further appealed that while giving larger counties mor representatives, smaller counties were left without representation.
(http://www.wvculture.org/history/statehood.html)

"Is that equality?" asked Harmon Sinsel of Taylor County, citing the populations of Cabell County, 7,000; Taylor County, 7,300; Greenbrier County, about 10,000 and Pocahontas County, 4,000 compared to smaller counties of 1,761 and 1,396. He went on to say that many of these counties "…away in the mountains after this rebellion is put down – their population will be less than it is now. Many of them will flee the country and never return. . . So I am opposed to increasing and to diminishing it." (http://www.wvculture.org/history/statehood.html)

Mr. Lamb called attention to the number of members that other states had fixed for the House of Delegates and pointed out that if the number forty-six were adopted, West Virginia would have the least house of any state in the Union except Delaware and Florida. (http://www.wvculture.org/history/statehood.html)

The convention opened on January 10, with the same disparity in giving each county at least one delegate. Mr. Van Winkle questioned the wisdom of such counties that could not afford to build its public buildings or pay the necessary taxes; and went on to say they should be willing to take the consequences. (http://www.wvculture.org/history/statehood.html)

Mr. Sinsel added, "What is Tucker, with 1,300 inhabitants that she should have one representative while others with a population of eight thousand and over only have one . . . but we are at the expense of a court in that county just as much as in the county of Ohio, and all the other judiciary when carried out; and add to that the expense of a separate representative. Why there will be nothing but a bill of expense any way you take them. And then the principle itself is unjust, unreasonable. I am opposed to it, utterly opposed to it." (http://www.wvculture.org/history/statehood.html)

A lawyer delegate from Tyler County, Abraham Soper, contended that the strong are always able to take care of the strong and that was an argument for allowing the smaller counties with less population a representative in the House of Delegates. "Have they not got an equal representation on this floor and in this body? Why is it? It is

because they represent a county organization? We have nothing to
do with the wisdom which created that organization. That we have
no business to inquire into; it is a matter that belongs to the people
themselves; because their small number of population brings any
increase of taxation upon them, that is a matter for them without any
fault to be found on our hand."
(http://www.wvculture.org/history/statehood.html)

Mr. Van Winkle alleged, "The difficulty is that it brings an
increase of taxation on the rest of us."
(http://www.wvculture.org/history/statehood.html)

"Well, now, sir," Soper fired back, "Let us look at that for a
moment. We have here a session to last forty-five days, and a
delegate comes from Tucker containing 1,400 inhabitants, and he
receives his three dollars a day – a little over one hundred dollars
Will gentlemen come up here and talk about the expenditure of a
paltry hundred dollars and find fault – the county of Ohio and others
find fault with that paltry sum because a county of equal
organization has a representative in the House of Delegates? It is too
insignificant to be taken into consideration at all." Mr. Soper went
on, "I have noticed in the papers that there is an application before
the legislature to permit a portion of the people of Preston to take a
vote on the propriety of being annexed to Tucker county, by which, I
do not know how greatly, but if it prevails there must be some equity
in it or the application would not be made – she probably may come
in with a respectable number of population...we are about to
organize our new State and we have invited every county to send
here a delegate for the purpose of expressing the views of the people
of that county; and I want, if we can organize our new State; that
every one of those counties shall have a representative in the house
of delegates. I believe it to be right and just that it should be so; and
I believe, sir, that it is according to the principle, which has been
adopted probably in almost every state in the Union."
(http://www.wvculture.org/history/statehood.html)

Mr. Lamb addressed the house, "The five smallest counties, each of which have a number less than one-half of what would entitle a county to a delegate, it is proposed by the gentleman from Doddridge shall each have a delegate, thus giving five delegates for a population of 8,736. Mason County ...has a population of 8,752; and she becomes to one delegate also. Now, in this favored section of the country, one man, in these counties, counts exactly as much as five men in Mason. The Constitution of the United States allows five Negroes to count as much as three white men; but five men in Mason County only count as much as one man in Tucker. Now, Mr. President, go home to your constituents and tell them that you have adopted an expedient here by which a man in Mason is to be rated as but one-third of a Negro, and see if you do not have votes against your Constitution. Am I going to my constituents and tell them that a man in Ohio County is to count as much as one-third of a Negro and expect them to vote for this Constitution. No, Sir!"
(http://www.wvculture.org/history/statehood.html)

Apportioning representatives according to total population continued to be debated, and Tucker County was consistently used as an example because of its lesser population of 1,396. There were delegates determined that each county should have a representative; they pushed for a larger number of delegates to assign to the House, 54, 56 or 59. The opposition pressed for 46.

Mr. Pomeroy of Hancock County, stated, "If you would give to Tucker, for example, a member, why, then, one man in that county will count as much in the house of delegates as five men in some other counties. That would be carrying our charity towards those counties to a point that I am not willing to extend." Pomeroy continued, "But I do not believe it can be made clear that one man in Tucker is as good as five men in Brooke. He ought to have the same voice in the legislature they would have. If so, there is a great improvement in men by migrating in that direction, and I would advise my friends in Brooke to increase their value by migrating to Tucker." (http://www.wvculture.org/history/statehood.html)

Mr. Lamb: "Mr. President, there are twenty counties, which have a population of less than the ratio. To these it is proposed to give twenty members. The aggregate white population of these twenty counties is 72,751. If they are assigned a member each it will be one for every 3,637. The other twenty-four counties have a population of 231,682. If the proposition of the gentleman from Marion should carry they would have 39 delegates, or one for every 5,940. Here, then, is the shorthand of this proposition: that 5,940 men, citizens, in one section of the State are to count as much as 3,637 in another section of the State." Mr. Lamb continued, "This is not pointing out the extreme cases, but it is the general result. Comparing the twenty counties with the twenty-four counties. If you go to the extreme cases, you will find, for instance, that Kanawha County has just about ten times the population of Tucker. If Tucker gets one delegate, Kanawha ought to have ten. He gives Kanawha two. A white man in Kanawha is equal only to one-fifth a white man in Tucker. And this is the state of things, which under the operation of this system of regarding county lines instead of white population you are to attempt to engraft in the Constitution of this State! . . It is said this would be overshadowing the small counties, to annex them to an adjoining county to constitute a district. Why, sir, suppose Tucker and Randolph, for instance, constituted but one county instead of having a county line drawn between them. Could we say the people of that end of the county were overshadowed or rendered inconsequent in the elections for the county? If Tucker should be annexed to Randolph County, would not she have precisely the weight in the county elections and in all other elections which the number of their voters would entitle them to?"
(http://www.wvculture.org/history/statehood.html)

Benjamin Stevenson of Wood: "I wish to call your attention to the matter of revenue in these different counties. I will take, for example, Wood - and I get these figures from the Auditor's report. She paid in the year 1860 into the state treasury as taxes $20,684.65. Let me take Tucker for an example on the other side. Tucker County paid in the same year $2,147.18. Wood County has a population of 10,791, nearly eight times the population of Tucker and pays nearly ten times the revenue that Tucker does. And yet you propose to give Tucker almost as much power, or at least half as much, in the laying of these taxes and in the method of expending them, and in making the laws to govern the people who pay them, that you do the people in Wood." (http://www.wvculture.org/history/statehood.html)

Chapman Stuart of Doddridge County: "I represent the county of Doddridge; and because five men in that county are only equal to one man in Tucker that is no reason why I am going to oppose this Constitution. I have it in my power now if I choose to do it - I mean the Convention - to refuse to the county of Tucker this representation; but if we give up to her, it is the part of magnanimity on our part and it is not forced upon us. And because we choose to be generous towards three or four little counties in our State, is that a reason that we shall assign that our people should vote against the constitution, simply because we are magnanimous towards two or three little counties, when we have it in our power to keep the representation from these little counties? It is a matter of gratuity on our part. It is not sought to be forced upon us by those counties. I pray you from the county of Ohio to be reconciled."
(http://www.wvculture.org/history/statehood.html)

James Paxton of Ohio County: "Will the gentlemen allow me to ask whether he claims that it is right that Tucker, with a population less than 1,400 should have a representation equal to a county of 7,000?" (http://www.wvculture.org/history/statehood.html)

Mr. Soper responded: "I insist that this is a right because we have organized this Convention by admitting a delegate from Tucker claiming an equal right with every delegate on this floor. The right of the delegate from Tucker to be here is because the county of Tucker had an organization before this convention was called."
(http://www.wvculture.org/history/statehood.html)

James William Parsons of Tucker County: "I would feel truly glad if this question could be dispensed with. It appears Tucker has been the test of the Convention for several days. As one of the reasons why I should be glad if we could dispense with that question it has been so ably discussed. I would feel truly glad if this Convention could feel that it should give us a representative. We never have been represented, sir, when we belonged to Randolph. We lived in the extreme end of the county. The result was a representative was always selected from the town of Beverly or above that. We had to go some thirty miles for our county seat. One gentleman stated on this floor that new counties were made frequently to favor some rich man. That was not the case in Tucker. It was to benefit a number of citizens that they might not have so far to go to their county seat. Since we have been formed into a county the result has been that we never have had a representative from our end of the county. It has been a man living some thirty, forty, or fifty miles south of us; and the result has been they have never favored our county whatever. We have never got any of the advantages of the legislature. But yet we think it is just. My friend said he did not intend to go any further with us; believed I had left him. I for one feel like going no further. I am favorable to a new state. I want a new state under any circumstances. But I am prompted by the rule to do justice. I do hope that we may get through with the question, that Tucker may not be the text any longer." (http://www.wvculture.org/history/statehood.html)

Finally, it was resolved that Tucker County and Randolph County would form the fifth delegate district and the delegate would be chosen the first three terms from Randolph County and the fourth term from Tucker County. (http://www.wvculture.org/history/statehood.html)

The new constitution was approved in a unanimous vote by the delegates on February 18, 1862. It was then submitted to the voters on April 24, who overwhelming approved the constitution, 18,862 to 514. On June 20, 1863, West Virginia became the 35th state in the United States of America. (http://www.wvculture.org/history/statehood.html)
Note: The entire proceedings of the conventions that led to West Virginia statehood can be found online at www.wvculture.org/history/statehood.html.

CIVIL WAR

IMBODEN IN TUCKER COUNTY

Colonel John Daniel Imboden set out from Franklin, in Pendleton County, with 300 Confederate Partisan Rangers on August 14, 1862, on a raid through Randolph and Tucker counties. His purpose was two-fold, to destroy the Baltimore & Ohio Railway Bridge at Rowlesburg, and to capture a detachment of approximately forty Federals stationed at Abraham Parsons' mill that stood along the mill race in Parsons, where Billings Avenue starts up Quality Hill. (Fansler 194)

Abraham Parsons was sheriff of Tucker County and one of those that raised a Confederate flag over the St. George Courthouse in June. His mill was seized and used as a bivouac for Federal troops and Abraham Parsons was captured and imprisoned. (Fansler 194)

So that his presence might not be revealed to the Federals in advance, Imboden avoided the roads and trails as much as possible. Piloted by the notorious Confederate scout, Ezekiel Harper, he came over Allegheny Mountain from the Mouth of Seneca. Imboden advanced through the deep black forest, hacking a trail through the dense thickets and averaging a mere fifteen miles a day. When he reached Glady Fork, about twelve miles northeast of Beverly, he turned northward and followed that stream to its junction with the Dry Fork River, where he halted around sundown to prepare supper. Colonel Imboden resumed his advance to Parsons' mill, only twelve miles away, at around ten o'clock. He reached the mouth of Otter Creek at dawn, traveling only seven miles in the darkness. After fording the Black Fork River four times, he finally reached Parsons and surrounded the mill. Much to his displeasure, he learned that the Federals had fled down Cheat River shortly before his arrival. Fording the river four more times, he arrived in St. George to find that the Federals had fled from there as well, toward Rowlesburg. Fearing that superior forces would be encountered at Rowlesburg, Imboden returned to his camp in Pendleton County. (Fansler 194-195)

Two weeks later, Colonel Imboden reported his failure: "I afterwards learned that an old fool, a friend, who saw our route the day before, spoke of it to a Union man, who took the news to Beverly and thence a courier warned the post of my approach just in time for them to flee. It was too bad. About fifteen mounted men I had with me caught up with them and had a skirmish. No damage was done. My infantry was so broken down by twenty-four hours marching that I had to halt a few hours for rest and sleep. During our rest a scoundrel, a sharp, shrewd German, deserted, stole a mule and went to Beverly and disclosed my numbers and what he suspected of my plans. The Commandant at Beverly at once telegraphed to New Creek and 1,000 men were sent up to Rowlesburg. Not knowing these facts at the time, I moved on, as soon as my men could travel to Saint George. Here I got reliable information that the troops from New Creek had reached Rowlesburg. In a short time I also ascertained that they were marching upon Saint George and were only a few miles distant. I took from the post office such of the records of the bogus County court as I could conveniently carry. I have sent them to Governor Letcher. I took all the goods from the store of Solomon Parsons member of the Wheeling Convention and leader of the Lincolnites in Tucker, and left him a receipt for them. He and all the Union men of the county had fled that morning. I began to fall back up the river. Just in the edge of the village of Saint George, I was riding some distance ahead of my men and suddenly came upon Old John Snyder and one of the Parsonses, both armed with rifles. Parsons fled and I got into a fight with Snyder. Just as he was aiming at me with his long rifle, I fired at him with my revolver. He dropped his gun like a hot potato and leaned forward on the neck of his horse and escaped into the laurel. Pursuit was immediately made but he escaped. I have since learned from some refugees that I wounded him badly, though I fear not mortally. I had a fair shot at about fifty yards and aimed at his hips. We were bushwhacked half a day in Tucker, as we fell back from Saint George, by Union men, but the cowardly scoundrels went so far up in the mountains that they only hit one of my men, and he was but slightly wounded in the foot. When within five miles of Parsons' mill, my brother (Captain George W. Imboden) met me and reported a sharp skirmish he had on the Beverly road, near Corricks Ford, with a Yankee picket or advance guard. Things now began to look bad. I feared a force from Beverly might reach the mill before me and cut me off from the Dry Fork pass, in which event I would have been compelled to whip them, or take to the mountains, with the loss of my pack mules; so I pushed ahead for the mill and on arriving there found no enemy. I moved up Dry Fork and encamped for the night with my rear safe in a position to whip 1,000 men in front, should they pursue me. The next day I struck the wilderness again, and in three days reached Slaven's cabin at the foot of Cheat Mountain, on the Staunton-Parkersburg turnpike. We subsisted on potatoes and beef on most of the route, there being no flour or meal in the country." (Fansler 195-196)

Dr. Solomon Parsons' home and store were located one-half mile east of St. George where the St. George-Leadmine road crosses Lower Dry Run. A farmhouse built by Dr. Parsons' grandson, Solomon John Parsons, remains on the property. A few weeks before Imboden's first run into Tucker County, Solomon Parsons had received a large shipment of merchandise. He then sent a taunting message to Imboden, daring him to come and get it. Much to his chagrin, Imboden did "come and get it." (Fansler 196)

It was soon learned that Imboden's advance on St. George was not betrayed by a Union man as he was led to believe, but by the nineteen-year-old daughter of John Snyder. The Snyder home was in the vicinity of Imboden's route, near Harman. Mary Jane Snyder learned that Confederates were close by, so she rode swiftly that night to Parsons' mill to warn the Federal troops in time for them to retreat to Rowlesburg. Mary Jane was a sister of Sampson Snyder, who organized the notorious "Swamp Dragons." (Fansler 198)

Imboden's second raid through Randolph and Tucker countie began on November 7, 1862. With 310 mounted Partisan Rangers he set out from his camp on the South Branch in a dreadfu snowstorm with intent purpose to destroy the railway bridge a Rowlesburg. They halted around midnight at the base of th Allegheny Front Mountain, thirty-eight miles from St. George. Wit William Harper as their guide, they set out again at dawn. The crossed the mountains and passed down to Red Creek following treacherous trail worsened by the deep snow. The trail was so roug that by nightfall they had traveled fewer than twenty miles. A midnight, with the moon to guide them, they set out again in th blinding storm. At the eastern edge of Rosendorf, one of the mule rolled over the embankment into the Dry Fork River, with canno strapped on, but both were retrieved and the march went forward (Fansler 200-201)

Imboden reached St. George at daybreak on Sunday morning November 9th, and surrounded Captain William Hall and a Federa garrison of twenty-nine men who had taken up headquarters in th courthouse. A flag of truce was sent to demand the surrender However, the truce bearer was fired upon and wounded in the foo by a sentinel who then rushed to the courthouse and rang the alarm There was much excitement among the Yankees; and when Ha learned that he was surrounded, he cried, "Boys, take care of you Captain!" (Maxwell 340-341)

Captain Hall's Headquarters were located in the county clerk' office. The alarm sounded just as he sat down to breakfast. Afte the surrender Imboden, with true Southern hospitality, invited Ha and his fellow officers to join them for a hardy breakfas Meanwhile, outside, around the campfire, Imboden's troops ate wit Hall's men. (Maxwell 341-342)

Imboden offered honorable terms and Captain Hall accepted. Th Yankees were disarmed and permitted to depart in peace. Jame Swisher was the only one that escaped. Located some distance fron the courthouse when the alarm was given, he took off for Rowlesburg to spread the news. (Fansler 201)

Dr. Solomon Parsons, a fervent Union supporter, lived only a half-mile from St. George and was down in the field feeding his cattle when Imboden's raiders passed by. Convinced that the confederates were after him, Parsons fled toward the river, which he waded at the lower end of Wamsley's Island, and proceeded to climb the mountain beyond. Reconsidering, he re-crossed the river and ascended Lower Dry Run, wading the bed to avoid the deep snow. Solomon then crossed Location Ridge and headed to Cranberry Summit (Terra Alta) where he remained for several days. Once more the Rebels carried off a second shipment of merchandise from his store. Solomon was sixty-seven years of age when this event occurred. (Fansler 202)

About this time, Captain Horace Kellogg came into command of the Union forces in Tucker County and levied an unfair assessment on the Rebel citizens, in the name of Brigadier General Robert H. Milroy, commander of the West Virginia Brigade. The purpose of the assessment was to reimburse Dr. Parsons, Enoch Minear and others for property losses sustained in the Imboden raids. The Union men disapproved and had nothing to do with this. The amounts collected were ten times the value of losses incurred and based more proportionally on the intensity of their southern sympathies. Nicholas M. Parsons was assessed $500, William R. Parsons $700, and Abraham Parsons $800. These three men were relatives of Solomon Parsons. Rufus Maxwell was assessed $80. William D. Losh was assessed $8 and was forced to sell his Sunday pants to raise the money. (Fansler 204)

Most of the money was collected and paid to those that claimed it. But when Kellogg's "assessment" was revealed to his superiors, Captain Joseph A. Faris was sent to St. George with instructions to stop the practice and repay the money. (Maxwell 345)

BRIGADIER GENERAL
JOHN DANIEL IMBODEN, C.S.A.

John Daniel Imboden was born near Staunton, Virginia, on February 1[?] 1823. He had a typical childhood, attending school near Staunton. At ag[?] sixteen he attended Washington College (Washington & Lee University) i[?] Lexington, for two years but did not graduate.

Imboden taught school for a time at the Virginia Institute for th[?] Education of the Deaf, Dumb and Blind in Staunton. Although [?] competent teacher, he chose to study law. He maintained a law practice i[?] Staunton, where he was elected representative to the Virginia legislatur[?] for two terms.

When the Civil War broke out, Imboden was commissioned captain [?] the Staunton Artillery. On July 21, 1861, he commanded a battery [?] artillery at First Manassas, where he was wounded by a shell fragment.

Leaving the artillery, Colonel Imboden organized a cavalry comman[?] named the First Partisan Rangers who were re-designated the 62nd Virgin[?] Mounted Infantry. They fought with Major General Thomas [?] "Stonewall" Jackson in his Shenandoah Valley Campaign of 1862, fightin[?] in the battles of Cross Keys and Port Republic. When Jackson went t[?] Richmond, Imboden was left in the Valley to continue operations of hi[?] force there and in the mountains.

On January 28, 1863, Imboden was appointed Brigadier Genera[?] Imboden and Brigadier General William E. "Grumble" Jones led th[?] famous Jones-Imboden raid into northwestern Virginia that severed th[?] vital rail artery of the B&O Railroad. From April 20, to May 27, 186[?] Imboden marched his command of 3,400 men through northwester[?] Virginia destroying railroad bridges and gathering horses, mules, and cattl[?] for the Confederacy. Imboden's route carried him 400 miles in 37 day[?] Torrential spring rains and mud slowed their progress, but his forc[?] destroyed eight railroad bridges, captured over $100,000 worth of Feder[?] animals and supplies, and rounded up 3,100 cattle. His command did n[?] participate in the grand reviews at Brandy Station, but when the Army [?]

Northern Virginia marched northward to Pennsylvania, Imboden's men went along, serving as the Confederate rear guard.

Imboden's finest moment occurred during the retreat. Given the important task of commanding the Army of Northern Virginia's wagon train of thousands of wounded, Imboden performed admirably, fending off the Federal cavalry and protecting the supplies and the vast number of wounded men. On July 6th, he was trapped on the banks of the flooding Potomac River, and scratched together a defensive force consisting of his brigade, some artillery, and the Waggoner's. There, they defeated a combined force commanded by John Buford and Judson Kilpatrick, and saved the Confederate wagon train.

After Gettysburg, Imboden continued to command troops in the Shenandoah Valley region. His next remarkable deed was the surprise and capture of an entire Federal regiment, nearly five hundred men of the Ninth Maryland Infantry, at Charles Town, on October 18, 1863. After Grumble Jones was court-martialed, Imboden served as his second-in-command until Jones fell leading his men into battle at Piedmont in June 1864. Imboden then served under Lt. General Jubal Early in the operations against Major General Philip H. Sheridan in Sheridan's Shenandoah Valley Campaign in 1864.

John Imboden proved effective, both as an artillery officer, and also as a commander of partisan cavalry forces. In a time of great need, Imboden performed admirably at Williamsport, and saved the Army of Northern Virginia's supplies and wounded from capture. Robert E. Lee recognized the importance of Imboden's service during the retreat and paid him the appropriate compliment: "In passing through the mountains in advance of the column, the great length of the trains exposed them to attack by the enemy's cavalry, which captured a number of wagons and ambulances; but they succeeded in reaching Williamsport without serious loss. They were attacked at that place on the 6th by the enemy's cavalry, which was gallantly repulsed by General Imboden."

Imboden died at seventy-two years of age on August 15, 1895, in Damascus, Virginia. He is buried in the general's section of Hollywood Cemetery in Richmond. (http://stonewall.hut.ru/leaders/imbodenjd.htm)

ST. GEORGE AND HOLLY MEADOWS
CHURCHES

Once known as the Ann Eliza Methodist Episcopal Churc
North, the St. George United Methodist Church was the first churc
house in St. George. A wooden plaque above the front entranc
reads, "St. George United Methodist Church, Est. 1840."

It is uncertain who built the church. Master carpenter Daniel I
Dumire hailed from Leadmine and built many impressive structure
in the St. George community. However, he was born in 1834 an
would have been far too young for such an undertaking. The churc
was built of expertly hewed and fitted logs, ceiled and weathe
boarded. When the siding was replaced in 1991, the hewn lo
structure revealed some boards the width of a man's torso. Th
church continues to hold regular services and is situated along Mi
Run. (Fansler 441)

A lease for the Ann Eliza Methodist Episcopal Church North wa
made by Dr. Solomon Parsons of the county of Randolph and stat
of Virginia to William Ewin, James W. Parsons, Jonathan M
Parsons, Enoch Minear and Jacob Dumire, trustees and thei
successors for the use of the Methodist Episcopal Church o
December 15, 1844.

On November 17, 1868, Dr. Solomon Parsons made a deed fc
the Ann Eliza Methodist Episcopal Church North, to Sansome E
Parsons and other trustees, Jacob Dumire, Enoch Minear, Andrev
Pifer and D. K. Dumire.

There has been a question about the origin of the name of the St
George Church. Some records show "Ann Eliza," but the lease an
deed show "Annaliza." A plaque inside the church asserts that th
lady is Ann Eliza Ferguson Bonnifield Minear, but Cleta Long tel

us in her account that she was unable to verify that information. Reverend C. B. Davis, pastor of the St. George circuit 1951–1952, wrote that the church was named "Ann Eliza" for the wife of Enoch Minear because of her outstanding work for the church. Enoch Minear was married two times. He married Catherine Stalnaker on June 1, 1827, and they had a daughter Eliza Ann who was born on March 14, 1833. She would have been seven years of age when the church was named. His second wife was Mary Ann (Wiles) Gilmore, and they married September 22, 1835. Perhaps the church was named for Enoch Minear's wife and daughter, "Ann" "Eliza." While researching this book, I discovered many misspelled names in deciphering wills and deeds, which may also explain the spelling of "Annaliza." We may never learn the true origin of the name of the St. George Church. It is certain that the church was built largely by the efforts of Enoch Minear and Solomon Parsons. They were prominent citizens and outstanding workers in the St. George Church and community. (Long 124-125) (Fansler 111)
(Courtesy of Gladys J. Pifer and St. George United Methodist Church)
(http://www.genforum.familytreemaker.com/minear/messages/100.html)

In 1859, a second church was built in St. George, the Methodist Episcopal Church South. It was located in the field midway between the steel bridge over Cheat River and the Limestone Road. When the Methodist Episcopal Churches merged in 1939, this one closed and became a residence. It was indeed built by master carpenter Daniel L. Dumire. (Fansler 441-442)

It has been told that slaves were hidden in the attic of the Ann Eliza Methodist Episcopal Church North during the Civil War. As the church appears today, it would have been unreasonable for any person to be in the attic for an extended period of time. It was also rumored that the church had a balcony for Negroes to sit during church services. The views on slavery differed between the two churches in St. George. Ann Eliza Methodist Episcopal Church North was against slavery. This is confirmed by the fact that Dr. Solomon Parsons and his son, James W. Parsons, were opposed to slavery and would not have affiliated with a church that supported

slavery.   However, the Methodist Episcopal Church South hel
southern sympathies.   (Long 125)

The St. George United Methodist Church is believed to be one c
the oldest Methodist churches in West Virginia that holds regula
services. For more than 160 years this church has been home to th
St. George community.

The Bethel Methodist Episcopal Church in Holly Meadows wa
the first church built in Randolph County, Virginia, in 1824. It wa
built of logs and stood in the present Bethel Cemetery, next to th
road. The present cemetery was the churchyard and Bethel churc
had a gallery for Negroes.   When Tucker County separated fror
Randolph in 1856, it took Randolph's pioneer church. (Long 123, 125

James Parsons and his wife, Nancy (Rust) Parsons, donated on
acre for the Bethel Church. This was the first deed made for a churc
lot recorded in Randolph County. It transfers one acre with "all th
woods, ways, waters and privileges," to William Parsons, Isaa
Parsons, Solomon Parsons, James Tygart and John Tygart, trustee:
"in trust that they shall erect and build or cause to be erected an
built thereon a house or place of worship for the use of the Methodi:
Episcopal Church in the United States of America."   Fansler sai
"the Parsons family were numerous and owned most of the land i
the Holly Meadows." (Fansler 625-626)

Mary Katherine (Bonnifield) Swisher's journal portrayed th
Bethel Church in Holly Meadows: "There was a church calle
Bethel about four miles from our home on the Horseshoe, to which
went in later years. It was built about ninety years ago and I think
was the only one in a radius of perhaps thirty miles, though ther
were preaching places. The building was of hewn logs, a twelve
pane window on each side with panes of glass eight by ten inches. ,
gallery for the slaves. On the women's side were two benches wit
backs. The other benches had no backs, simply plain plank benche:
A small wood stove in the center completed the outfit. A moder
congregation would feel out of place in such a church. Old Uncl

Titus, a black man, made the fires in winter. In the spring he came around for his pay. All he asked was as much maple sugar as each family would give. The old church is gone but the cemetery in back is still used occasionally by those whose relatives have been buried there for several generations. Sunday School commenced at ten o'clock. The leader read a chapter, sang a hymn and led in prayer. Then all who could read stood up in a row and read verse about in the Testament. Those who could not read were taught in the spelling book. Then before dismissal all stood in a row again and spelling was given out as in weekday school. We had no Sunday School literature but Testaments and a few Tracts. Had the row of spellers at twelve o'clock, then we ate our lunch and enjoyed a social hour, then took Sunday School again for an hour or two. We got a pen written ticket for good behavior and one for every five verses of the Testament we committed to memory, during the week, and recited in Sunday School. For every five tickets we got a page of Tracts which we prized very much. It was easy to memorize and I often repeated whole chapters. Once I was at a meeting in Uncle Enoch Minear's stone house, where the preacher gave out a hymn, two lines at a time, as was the custom. The congregation stood up, turned their backs to the preacher and sang the lines. There was an advantage in the position of the worshipers. They were in a favorable position to kneel which they did, something becoming out of style now." (Fansler 626-627)

After fifty-three years of school and worship at Bethel Church, a new church was erected in 1877 across the road on a grassy knoll among a handsome grove of oak trees. It was named the Holly Meadows Presbyterian Church, but was called "The Bethel Church" throughout its existence. The first annual Parsons Family Reunion was held at the "Presbyterian White Oak" church, so named by the Parsonses, and continued there until 1968.
(Fansler 627-628) (MacCabe 286)

FIRST PARSONS FAMILY REUNION 1907

"The first annual Parsons' Family Reunion was held at the Presbyterian White Oak church, in Tucker County, West Virginia on July 28, 1907. The committee on arrangements made a bower of the place by decorating it with ferns, cypress, wild Indigo and flowers which grew in the woods nearby.

Before ten o'clock the people began to arrive in hacks, buggies, road wagons and horse-back, while those nearby, walked. One hundred and fifty names were enrolled, all Parsons or related by marriage. At eleven o'clock the exercises were opened by organ; voluntary prayer by Solomon J. Parsons of St. George; anthem by choir; opening address "Pioneer life of the Parsons" by Leland S. Parsons, of Oakland, California; a solo by Hazel Hulings of Parsons, duet by Pearl and Nellie Long; recitations by Martha Parsons and Mrs. C.W. Minear; Miss Mary Kathryn Minear presided at the organ and conducted the exercises. Dinner was announced and a recess was taken. . .

Some had not met for twenty years and they enjoyed talking over the days of long ago. The Thomas concert band was present and entertained with some splendid music, which added much pleasure to the occasion. In the afternoon some wills were read by Mrs. J.S. Brown. The Hon. J. Slidell Brown of Kingwood, West Virginia was called to the speaker's stand and delivered a fine address; he said it was worth traveling fifty miles to get a seat in the middle of the well loaded table where he could reach both ways. . .

It was voted to hold the annual reunion the third Saturday of August. The following officers were elected: President, Solomon J. Parsons; Vice-President, Joseph Parsons; Secretary Bascom B. Parsons; Historian, Minnie Parsons; Assistant, M.K. Minear. They adjourned and everyone went home feeling happy and hoping to meet again the next year. . ." (MacCabe 286-287)

CHURCH LEASE 1844

Dr. Solomon Parsons
To
Trustees of Methodist Episcopal Church

Know all men by these present that I Solomon Parsons of the County of Randolph and State of Va lease the Annaliza Church at the mouth of "Mill Run" unto Wm Ewin, James W. Parsons, Jonathan M. Parsons, Enoch Minear and Jacob Dumire, Trustees, in trust, and their successors for the use of the Methodist Episcopal Church, to have, hold and enjoy all the right and privileges and have free and full and peaceable possession of said church with the same right and privileges that is given to Trustees in the discipline of the Methodist Episcopal Church the same as though it was deeded as long as it is used by the Methodist Episcopal Church as a regular preaching place and should they the Methodist Episcopal Church cease to use it as a place to regularly preach in then and not until then this lease shall be null and void and the said church return to me and my heirs. In witness I set my hand and affix my seal this 15th day of December 1844.
Solomon Parsons. (Seal)

State of West Virginia
On this 17th day of May 1866, this lease was produced to me John J. Adams Recorder, with and for the county of Tucker in my office and admitted to record.

CHURCH DEED 1868

Dr. Solomon Parsons
To
Sansome E. Parsons and others, Trustees

This Deed, made the seventeenth day of November in the Year o
Our Lord, One Thousand Eight Hundred and Sixty-Eight, betweer
Solomon Parsons of Portland, Preston County, State of Wes
Virginia, of the first part, and Sansome E. Parsons, Jacob Dumire
Enoch Minear, Andrew Pifer and D.K. Dumire of Tucker County
and State aforesaid, Trustees of the M.E. Church at St. George, o
the second part. Witnesseth: that in consideration of the sum of One
Dollar, the receipt of which is hereby acknowledge, the said party o
the first part do grant unto the said parties of the second part, the
following described property, that is to say, one piece or parcel o
land, lying above or N. W. of the Town lots, as laid out East of Mil
Run on the lands of Dr. Solomon Parsons, and recorded in Deed
Book No.- 1, Page 90, as (undecipherable) of said lots in the town o
St. George. Beginning at a point at the said Town lots and running a
straight line from line of the said lots ten feet below the Church (tha
is thereon erected and known as "Analiza" M. E. Church) to Mil
Run, thence with the meanderings of said Run, to the "Old Mill Rur
Road" that crosses said Run, thence with said Road to the N. line o
upper line of the above mentioned lots, thence with said N. line, o
upper line to the point above mentioned, or beginning point
(Running a straight line from the upper line of said Town Lots to
Mill Run, being ten feet below, or west of said Church), and the
party of the first part hereby convey the said piece or parcel of land
to the parties of the second part, as Trustees of said Church and to
their successors, and the said party of the first part do hereby
covenant with the said parties of the second part that he will warran
and defend specially the property hereby conveyed. Witness the
following signature and seal,
Solomon Parsons (Seal)

WILL OF SOLOMON PARSONS

I, Solomon Parsons of the County of Preston and State of West Virginia, Being advanced to old age, and being of sound mind, and disposing memory and desiring to make a distribution of what property my Heavenly Father has blessed me with, make and publish this as my last will and testimony, in the following manner. First, I direct my executor to pay all my just debts and funeral expenses, and to have erected a tombstone similar to the one erected for my wife. Second. I give and bequeath to Hellen (Helen) L. Parsons daughter of my son James Two hundred (200.00) dollars. Third, I give and bequeath to Dianah (Diana) Shaan (Shahan) wife of John Shaan (Shahan) all of my bedding, bed and bedstead. Fourth I give and bequeath the residence after paying the just debts and expenses provided for in this will to Rebecca A. Elliott, wife of William Elliott. I hereby exclude James W. Parsons and Dianah (Diana) Parsons from any participation in any of my property they having secured from me in my lifetime their full share of my estate. I hereby constitute and appoint J.P. Jones of Portland as my executor not doubting his endeavor to carry out the provisions of this my last will and testament in writing whereof I have hereunto set my hand and seal in my hand as and for my last will at Portland Preston County State of West Virginia this 24th day of March A.D. 1875, signed in the presence of each other.

Solomon Parsons (Seal)
Joseph Jackson, John W. Watson
(Rebecca Parsons Elliott is a daughter; Helen Parsons Miller and Diana Parsons Shahan are granddaughters)

Chapter VIII

JAMES WILLIAM PARSONS

James William Parsons and Catherine (Neville) Parsons

Catherine A. Neville (first marriage)
Married: May 29, 1832
Nine Children: Jane Rebecca (Parsons) Wheeler, Mortimore (Died in infancy), Sansome E., Hannah Agnes (Parsons) Parsons, Mary, Helen Louise (Parsons) Miller, Anne Amelia (Parsons) Pifer, Solomon John and Diana Elizabeth (Parsons) Shahan (MacCabe 242)

Ann Eliza Prentis (second marriage)
Married: May 17, 1859
(MacCabe 242)

James William: Born January 13, 1813, Randolph County, Virginia
Died February 1, 1892, Preston County, West Virginia
(Dates taken from the grave marker, Maplewood Cemetery, Kingwood, West Virginia)

Catherine A. Neville: Born June 23, 1808
Died February 22, 1858
(Date of birth, Judy Greek) (Date of death, MacCabe 242)

Ann Eliza Prentis: Born April 9, 1811
Died August 19, 1890, Preston County, West Virginia
(Grave marker, Maplewood Cemetery, Kingwood, West Virginia)

James William Parsons is the paternal grandfather of Worley Parsons.

James W. Parsons is the lone son of Dr. Solomon and Hannah (Parsons) Parsons and was born January 13, 1813, in the Horseshoe in Randolph County, Virginia. He was reared on the home plantation and engaged in farming. His first wife was Catherine Neville, the daughter of John and Margaret (Green) Neville, and nine children blessed this union. His second wife was Ann Eliza Prentis. (MacCabe 242) (Nevilles, Courtesy of Judy Greek)

The Parsons house stood on a bluff overlooking the Cheat River. MacCabe wrote, "…like most Virginia homes it was celebrated from its earliest days for the most graceful and openhanded hospitality, it was the land of plain living, high thinking, the abode of simplicity and democracy." (243)

James was a devoted member of the Methodist Episcopal Church North. Politically, he was an influential member of the Republican Party, and by following in the footsteps of his father, Dr. Solomon Parsons, he served as a delegate to the Constitutional Convention for the new state of West Virginia from 1861 to 1863. (MacCabe 242)

" 'In 1769, Christopher Neugen settled somewhere in the Holly Meadows, lived there for awhile and sold his claim to James Riddle and Joseph Hardman, who had come with the group of colonists led by John Minear. Neugen then disappeared from the area. Riddle and Hardman traded the land to George H. Long for a pair of silver knee buckles and a forty-dollar horse, after which they, too, disappeared from the area. There is a long standing legend that Neugen buried a pot of gold under a large boulder on his farm. The story goes that he was a thief and probably stole the gold, hence his reason for hiding it. For years Holly Meadows farmers plowed with enthusiasm in the hope of finding the boulder under which the gold had been hidden. Some years later it was learned that Neugen had been hanged in Richmond, Virginia, for a capital offense, supposedly murder. . .' " The legend comes from a manuscript prepared by Ogdie Beatrice (Poling) Long where she sited her information as being provided by James W. Parsons and Virginia Parsons MacCabe. (Fansler 57)

In 1860, James retired from business, divided his land among his children, and moved to Kingwood, (West) Virginia. (MacCabe 242) Jane Rebecca Parsons was the eldest daughter of James and Catherine Parsons. Born on June 13, 1833, in a Christian home surrounded by good influence, Jane grew to womanhood and was considered one of the most attractive girls of the period.
(MacCabe 243) (Birth date, Courtesy of Judy Greek)

Jane married David Wheeler on March 6, 1851, and they had eight children. She passed away suddenly on March 5, 1865, following the birth of her eighth child, Jane Rebecca "Jennie."
(MacCabe 243) (Wheeler family, Courtesy of Judy Greek)

James Parsons provided a loving home for his granddaughter who married Dr. Samuel Pratt on August 13, 1884. Jennie then cared for her grandfather Parsons in his waning years, following the death of his beloved wife, Ann Eliza. (MacCabe 243)
(Wheeler family, Courtesy of Judy Greek)

James W. Parsons and his second wife, Ann Eliza, are interred within the "old section" of the Maplewood Cemetery, Kingwood, West Virginia. A beautiful monument was erected for the Parsonses by their granddaughter.

SANSOME ELLIOTT PARSONS

Sansome Elliott Parsons is the second son of James W. Parsons and Catherine (Neville) Parsons and was born October 30, 1838, in the Horseshoe, Virginia. He married Adeline Elmira Parsons (1831-1910) on December 12, 1864, and they had five children: Etta Irene, Arthur W., Edgar Joseph, James M., and Clayton N. (http://www.rootsweb.com/~wvtucker/mgs.htm) (MacCabe 244) (Grave markers, Bethel Cemetery, Holly Meadows, West Virginia)

His residence stood on an elevation overlooking the Cheat River bottom, on or near the site of the first stockade fort, at the county farm. His grandfather, Dr. Solomon Parsons, had inherited the land from his father, Captain James Parsons. The Horseshoe farm was one of the oldest and finest in Tucker County; part of it was under cultivation for over one hundred years. It contained 174 acres of which 150 acres were highly improved. Besides the Horseshoe farm, Sansome owned nearly 4,000 acres of land in different parts of the county. (Maxwell 35, 93, 476-477)

In addition to farming, Sansome E. Parsons was an influential man who held several county offices that included: Commissioner, county court, county treasurer, and commissioner of schools. He was also an incorporator of the St. George Academy and trustee of the Methodist Episcopal Church North. (Maxwell 477) (Fansler 231, 243, 437)

Before the town of Parsons was incorporated, it had a post office named "Job" for the aged Job Parsons Sr. It was located in the Cheat River Hotel where the present-day courthouse stands and Sansome Parsons was the postmaster there from 1889-1893. (Fansler 382)

The timber that was sawed into lumber in Tucker County wa taken to market down the river in rafts to Rowlesburg. An averag raft contained seventy logs, which were bound together by pole fastened across the logs by staples. The oars, which were from twenty to fifty feet long, were placed on the ends of the rafts to kee them in the channel. Each year a large number of log rafts wen down the Cheat River. Sansome Parsons was among the most-note raftsmen along the river. (Maxwell 162)

During the Civil War, Sansome Parsons supported the Unio cause. When the Confederates left Tucker County in June 1861 following Lieutenant McChesney's death, they captured Sansom Parsons and William Hebb. Bound together, the men were taken t Rich Mountain, and when Garnett's army retreated, he carried ther along. The night they passed up the head of Leadmine Run, Parson untied himself and leaped over an embankment. Even though man shots were fired, he was able to escape unharmed. (Maxwell 477 (Fansler 168)

Camp Kidd, located on the county farm and six miles from Parsons, was developed in 1939, when the Works Progres Administration built a huge dairy barn on the property. It was name for Arnett L. Kidd who was the county agent between 1941 an 1948. The Holly Meadows Country Club leased 240 acres of th farm including the dairy barn that was renovated into a clubhouse The property is the former Sansome E. Parsons farm, which he sol to the county on April 9, 1891, for a poor farm. (Fansler 67€ Following a logging accident, Sansome built a home in Parsons West Virginia, where he resided until his death on June 5, 1903. (MacCabe 244)

WILL OF ANN ELIZA (PRENTIS) PARSONS

In the name of God. Amen.

I, Ann Eliza Parsons, of the town of Kingwood, County of Preston and State of West Virginia, do make this my last will and testament, hereby revoking all other former wills by me heretofore at any time made:

1st. I desire that my body be decently buried without needless expense and that my executor having after named procure a suitable tombstone to mark my resting place.

2nd. I give and bequeath all my property both real and personal to my adopted daughter Jennie Pratt, wife of Dr. S.H. Pratt, subject to the following charge upon the said real estate, to wit: That the said Jennie Pratt shall comfortably maintain, clothe and support my husband, James W. Parsons so long as he may choose to continuously make his home with her upon that part of said real estate situated in the town of Kingwood.

3rd. I appoint Dr. S.H. Pratt the sole executor of this my will and I desire that he shall not be required to give security upon his qualification as such executor. To Mary E. (undecipherable) I here leave my blessing having provided for her in another way.
Witness my hand this 1st day of September 1884.
Ann E. Parsons.

Two codicils were dated January 19, 1885 and February 17, 1886.

Chapter IX

SOLOMON JOHN PARSONS

Solomon John Parsons and Emma (Parsons) Parsons

Married: June 24, 1869
Six children: Prentis M., Hattie (Parsons) Hahn, Arthur Wilbur Marvin, Truman, and Worley
(MacCabe 246)

Solomon John: Born October 18, 1848, Randolph County, Virginia
Died December 10, 1926, Tucker County, West Virginia
(MacCabe 246)

Emma R.: Born July 16, 1850, Randolph County, Virginia
Died March 23, 1938, Tucker County, West Virginia
(MacCabe 246)

Solomon John Parsons and Emma are interred at St. George Cemetery, St. George, West Virginia.

Solomon John Parsons descended from Captain James Parsons, and Emma (Parsons) Parsons descended from the elder Parsons brother Thomas Parsons Jr.

Solomon John Parsons is the third son of James W. Parsons and Catherine A. (Neville) Parsons. He was born October 18, 1848, in the Horseshoe, Virginia. He married Emma (Parsons) Parsons on June 24, 1869, and they had six children. (MacCabe 246)

Solomon Parsons' vocation was farming; his farm was stocked with the best horses and cattle. When James W. Parsons divided his land among his children in 1873, he deeded two tracts of land to his son Solomon that amounted to four hundred acres. One hundred acres was well cultivated and three hundred acres were not so well improved. The property is located a mere one-half mile east of St. George, West Virginia, where the farmhouse remains.

Solomon Parsons was considered one of the best hunters in Tucker County while he followed the sport. In the fall of 1870, along with Charles L. Parsons and Sansome E. Parsons, he killed thirty-one deer. It was during one such hunting expedition that he met with an accident that proved nearly fatal. Solomon and Charles Parsons were hunting along the bluff near Sims' Bottom when Solomon accidentally fell over a cliff, approximately eighty-five feet, striking several projecting rocks, and plummeted two hundred feet further into Cheat River. Charles Parsons dragged Solomon, unconscious, from the river and saved him from drowning. Fortunately, he recovered in a relatively short time. (Maxwell 474)

Charles L. Parsons was a farmer who lived three miles from St. George on Jonathan Run, land that he had inherited from his uncle George H. Parsons and part of the original Isaac Parsons land. He and Solomon were distant cousins. Charles lost his left arm in 1874 in an accident involving a thrashing machine. (Maxwell 474)

EMMA (PARSONS) PARSONS

Emma R. Parsons is the daughter of Job Parsons Sr. and Job's second wife, Sarah (Losh) Parsons (1810-1902). Emma' maternal grandparents are Gedry Stephen Losh (1779-1875) and Sarah (Dashner) Losh (1771-1856). (MacCabe 43)   (Fansler 526 (Gravesites at St. George Cemetery, St. George, West Virginia) (Gravesit Stephen and Sarah Losh in the woods off Maxwell Run in Tucker County, Wes Virginia.)

Stephen Losh is the son of John Adam and Susannah Losh, and he was born in Morgormay Township, Northumberland County Pennsylvania, on August 29, 1779. He married Sarah Dashner abou 1795, and she is the daughter of George and Sarah Dashner o Philadelphia, Pennsylvania. They were the parents of six children Mary, Elizabeth, William, Anna, Catherine, and Sarah.
(Fansler 526, 643)

The family was German Lutherans, and he was christened "Gedr: Stephen Losh" but never used the name Gedry. Stephen brought hi family to Randolph County from Rockingham County, Virginia, i 1815. He built a makeshift shanty on Horseshoe Run and lived o fishing, hunting and trapping, while his wife and children worked th fields and harvested the crops. He later built a cabin of buckeye log at the mouth of Maxwell Run on the Seneca Trail. A tenant of eithe James or Thomas Parsons had previously lived on the land.
(Fansler 643)

Soon after settling, he learned the land belonged to Isaac Parsons son of James Parsons. He moved again, a mile down Horseshoe Rur to the mouth of Mike or Hansford Run, only to learn the lane belonged to Michael Hansford. Losh then moved three miles u Horseshoe Run and settled at the mouth of Hile Run. This place came to be known as the "Losh Place." But Stephen lost the place in a lawsuit and was forced to spend the remainder of his days living with friends and relatives. Sarah died January 11, 1856, and Stephen

died shortly before his 95th birthday on June 13, 1875. Both are buried north of Maxwell Run, off the Horseshoe road, in a little cemetery in the woods, overlooking the site of his buckeye cabin. Losh was a wagon master in the War of 1812 and served mostly in the Carolinas. "Wagon Master, wife and family" appears on his grave marker. (Fansler 643)
(Gravesites on Maxwell Run, Tucker County, West Virginia)

Fansler tells us: ". . . He was the "Davy Crockett" of Tucker County. He was an expert swimmer and swam flooded Cheat River several times when others feared to cross it with a boat or raft. He once swam the Cheat, just below Slip Hill where David Bonnifield drowned, when it was unusually high, against the advice and counsel of all his friends, who, when it was apparent that he could not be persuaded to abandon his foolhardy plan, gathered at the river bank to watch him die and do what they could to recover his corpse. It was evening and the shades of night made it so dark the opposite shore could not be seen when Stephen Losh stripped off his clothing (all he wore were shirt, shoes and trousers), wrapped it in his buckskin shirt, tied the bundle to his back, and plunged into the muddy river. A half hour elapsed during which the watchers could see nothing and hear nothing but the wash of the waters, and they were certain that Losh had perished when his mocking laughter came to them from the opposite shore. He visited someone on that side of the river and the next evening swam back across the Cheat." (644)

DECENDANTS OF
SOLOMON AND EMMA PARSONS

Prentis M. Parsons was born September 25, 1870, and marrie Mary Goff in 1897. They had five children: Margaret, Henriett Emma, Solomon J., and Diana. Prentis moved to Nebraska durin his early years and never returned to Tucker County. (MacCabe 247)

Hattie Parsons was born March 23, 1873, and married W. Hahn on May 16, 1894. She passed away on March 27, 1947. The had six children: Edward J., Olive Marie, Hattie Hazel, Emma S Margaret A. and William Parsons Hahn. (MacCabe 247)

Arthur Wilbur "Nick" Parsons was born December 15, 1875. H married Hurley Parsons, and they had seven children: Arthur B Solomon J., Nicholas C., Hattie Louise, Van Howard, Prentis, an Fred Parsons. (MacCabe 248)

Marvin Parsons was born May 31, 1879, and married Amy M Lipscomb on December 25, 1898. They had eleven children: Clyd Earl, Maurice Vernon, Fred Leslie, Ethel Irene (Parsons) Knott Edith Virginia (Parsons) Poiteveint, Gerald Marvin, John Hank Helen Elaine (Parsons) Ferguson, Eric Boyce, Mary Paulin (Parsons) Cross, and Ruth Eleanor (Parsons) Cade. Amy passe away in 1879 and Marvin in 1964. (MacCabe 248) (Gravesites, St. Georg Cemetery, St. George, West Virginia) (Courtesy of Marvin E. Parsons and Ali Parsons Phillips)

A son Truman was born December 13, 1880, and lived but on year. He passed away on December 31, 1881. (MacCabe 246)

Worley Parsons is the youngest son of Solomon J. Parsons an Emma R. (Parsons) Parsons. (MacCabe 246)

WILLIAM PARSONS HAHN

William Parsons "Bill" Hahn is the son of Hattie (Parsons) Hahn and W. T. Hahn, and was born on February 1, 1913, at Hambleton, West Virginia. William was preceded in death by his first wife, Melba Rea Hahn, and was survived by his second wife, Blanche E. (Wolford) Hahn. He had two sons, William D. Hahn and Jack E. Hahn, three step-daughters; seven grandchildren; six step-grandchildren; and two step-great-grandchildren. William is the grandson of Solomon John and Emma Parsons.

A 1931 graduate of Parsons High School, William earned his bachelor's degree at Shepherd College and his master's at West Virginia University. He taught and coached football at Spencer, Piedmont, Ridgeley, Fort Hill and Wheaton high schools.

In 1942, he coached the Fort Hill, Maryland, football team to a seven-one-one record before enlisting in the United States Navy. While serving during World War II, Lieutenant Hahn received the Victory Ribbon and the World War II American Area Campaign Ribbon. He was discharged on October 19, 1946. William returned to Fort Hill to coach the football and track teams, leading the 1946 football Sentinels to a five-one-two record. He taught and coached at Fort Hill for twelve years before leaving Cumberland, Maryland, to teach and coach at Wheaton High School.

Hahn directed Fort Hill to fourteen straight winning seasons, compiling a 110-thirteen-seven record. His teams were twenty-six-one-two in City League games and won thirteen straight championships. Fort Hill played twenty-seven consecutive City League games without a loss. Under Coach Hahn, Fort Hill had two eighteen game winning streaks and four undefeated seasons. The greatest team Jim Tatum ever coached at Maryland had seven Fort Hill guys on it. William Parsons Hahn passed away on August 13, 2000. (*The Parsons Advocate*, September 6, 2000)   (MacCabe 247)

OLIVE MARIE (HAHN) LIPSCOMB

Olive Marie Hahn was the daughter of W. T. and Hattie (Parsons) Hahn, and granddaughter of Solomon John and Emma (Parsons) Parsons of St. George, West Virginia. Marie was born on March 21, 1899. (MacCabe 247)

The first school in Hambleton was a one-room building on Fourth Street, which Marie attended until the eighth grade. In 1918, Marie graduated from Black Fork District High School, which became Parsons High School in 1933, when a county unit school system was inaugurated. She graduated from Shepherd College with a degree in elementary education and began her teaching career at Hambleton Grade School. Marie Hahn was the mayor of Hambleton for two consecutive terms, 1927-1928 and 1928-1929.   (Fansler 297, 389)

Soon after the death of her mother, Marie moved to Jarrettsville, Harford County, Maryland, in 1948. She met Ray Lipscomb, a native of St. George, West Virginia, and nephew of her uncle, Marvin Parsons. After they were married, Marie and Ray managed a poultry farm at White Hall, a short distance from Jarrettsville.

Marie taught at the Jarrettsville Graded School until her retirement in the late 1960s. She was very active in community and church. Marie (Hahn) Lipscomb faithfully attended the Parsons Family Reunions and was responsible for the second printing of *MacCabe's Parsons Family History and Record.* Her date of death is unknown.   (Courtesy of Marvin E. Parsons)

DEED

James W. Parsons to Solomon J. Parsons 1873

This deed made the 13th day of October in the year of our Lord one thousand eight hundred and seventy-three, between James W. Parsons and Ann Eliza Parsons-his wife of Preston County in the state of West Virginia grantors of the first part and Solomon J. Parsons of the County of Tucker in the state aforesaid, grantee and party of the second part. Witnesseth: that in consideration of the sum of Five dollars, the receipt of which is hereby acknowledged, and the higher and greater consideration of love and affection. The said grantors doth grant to the said grantee the following property, that is to say, two tracts of land, situate in the county of Tucker – in the state aforesaid to wit: one tract of 147 1/4 acres, being the tract on which the grantee now resides, it being the upper end of the old Salathiel Goff Survey of 250 acres on the east side of Cheat River and at the mouth of Dry Run and is bounded as follows …Also one tract of 252 acres adjoining the above described tract, which tract of 252 acres was granted by the Commonwealth of Virginia to the grantor- James W. Parsons and is bounded as follows… And the said James W. Parsons and _____ Parsons, his wife, do hereby covenant with the said party of the second part that they will warrant specially the property hereby conveyed. Witness the following signatures and seals.

James W. Parsons
Ann Eliza Parsons
Recorded in Deed Book No. 3-Page 155
The Records of Tucker County

WILL OF SOLOMON JOHN PARSONS

I, Solomon J. Parsons, of St. George, in the County of Tucker, State of West Virginia, declare this to be my last will and testament:

I.   I give and bequeath to the children of my deceased son, Prentiss M. Parsons, the sum of $5.00 each.

II.   I give and bequeath to my beloved wife, Emma Parsons, all of my personal property, of every kind and character, including moneys, notes, household and kitchen furniture, and my one-half interest in all live stock and farming machinery, implements and utensils, owned jointly by my son Worley Parsons and myself (after the payment of any just debts owing by me at the time of my death, funeral expenses, and the bequests hereinbefore made).

III.   I give and devise to my son, Worley Parsons, all of my real estate, including my home farm and the adjacent upland, situate near the village of St. George, in Tucker County, West Virginia, for and during the period of his natural life time, and after his death to his children; it being my will and purpose, by the provisions contained in this paragraph, that my said son, Worley Parsons, shall have a life estate in all my said real estate, with remainder to his children.

IV.   Having heretofore made advancements to my other living children, as stated following: To my son, A.W. Parsons, the sum of $500.00; to my son, Marvin Parsons, certain real estate, heretofore conveyed by deed to him; and to my daughter, Hattie Hahn, the sum of $500.00 and other personal property; it is, therefore, my will that they shall receive nothing further from or out of my estate, either real or personal, and accordingly no further provision is made for them, or either of them, in this my will.

V.   I appoint my said, son, Worley Parsons, executor of this my will.

In Witness Thereof, I, Solomon J. Parsons, have to this my last will and testament subscribed my name and set my seal, this the 11th day of April 1925.

WILL OF EMMA (PARSONS) PARSONS

St. George, West Va
Sept. 12, 1932
I, Emma Parsons in sound mind do hereby bequest
to my Daughter Hattie Lucas my spare rug and all
pertaining to the suit and all my clothes and
evrything in my dresser in my room and to my son
Marvin I give him my bed and beding that goes
with it and my red lounge and to Willes I give him
his fathers clock that is (in) the dining room and to
my son Worley Parsons I give the dresser that is in
his room and the 184 dollars he borrowed of me to
pay taxes and to Mirea Hahn the old grandfathers
clock and I want her to stratten up expences and
what money if any is left she is to keep it and I
want the balance of my things divided among all my
children and if they cant agree make a sale and sell
them and the ones raises a fuss he neednt have any
thing for I don't want any fussing for my things

(Handwritten and unsigned will of Emma Parsons was transcribed as written)

ST. GEORGE, WEST VIRGINIA

In 1776, a hearty band of about forty settlers followed John Minear across the mountains from Moorefield, Virginia, to establish a rugged existence along the Cheat River. An exact figure is unknown of the number of men, women and children who came to the beautiful hills of West Virginia that Captain Parsons had discovered when he struggled to return to the South Branch after being captured by Indians. (Fansler 423)

A mountain barrier prevented most means of travel, so they came walking, leading their cattle and packhorses, and carrying their young. The journey was difficult even for the Indians who were skilled in navigating the tangled forest. But the white man was even more challenged, for he had horses, cattle and household goods. (Fansler 423)

The group had either sold or given away their heavy furniture and unmanageable belongings, before leaving Moorefield. They brought with them only the bare necessities, wooden and pewter cooking utensils, iron skillet and kettle, dough tray, water jug, axe, rifle, bedclothes, homespun clothing and a few carpenter tools. (Fansler 423)

As they moved westward, the cattle and packhorses lived off the land. Mothers carried their infants, and small children were placed in baskets, tied together like saddlebags, and carried by packhorses. The older children led the cattle and horses, filled the water jugs, and gathered wood for the campfire. (Fansler 423-424)

After sundown, a fire was kindled and a meal prepared, often of bear meat, venison and corn bread. The meat was roasted on coals or spits, and the bread was baked in ash ovens or skillets. They slept on bearskins and quilts under the stars; and if it rained, they built bark shelters. The cattle and horses were turned loose to fend for themselves. At first light, they had a pan of corn porridge and continued on their journey. (Fansler 424)

Their first priority upon arrival at St. George, was building a fort for protection from the Indians and homes for the colonists. The first homes were particularly crude structures, often without windows and floors, as they were constructed with the materials at hand. Later on, when a sawmill and materials were available, a more substantial dwelling was generally built. The house was made of logs, usually one story, and sometimes with a loft. They had no nails. Even the door hinges and latches were resourcefully constructed. The first chimneys were quite a fire hazard, as they were built on the inside of the dwelling. The fire was directly beneath the chimney so that the smoke and sparks could escape. If a floor existed, it was made of split logs with the flat side up, called puncheon. Small holes in the walls served the twofold purpose of admitting light and shooting game or the Indians. A single door was made of heavy bulletproof slabs and held together by transverse pieces. It was secured with a bar across the inside against invasion. (Fansler 424-425)

The furniture was plain but adequate. The bedsteads were crude frames, and the beds consisted of animal skins and bed ticks filled with dried grass or straw. Lice that sometimes got into these were also called "bed ticks." Tables and benches were rough slabs on pegs. (Fansler 425)

The first people in St. George wore garb of deerskin trousers and skirts and deer skin coats, called hunting shirts. The edges and facing of the coats were decorated with fringes. Fringes similarly extended down the outside of each trouser leg and around the hems of skirts. The fastenings were either leather thongs or homemade buttons. Like the Indians, they wore deerskin moccasins that were cut in one piece and closed by a drawstring above the ankles. The tops were extended in two long flaps that were wrapped around the legs for further protection. Drying the feet each night before the fire was essential. Socks were not worn but frequently leaves were stuffed into the moccasins for warmth. Usually a fur cap was worn, made from raccoon skin with the animal's tail hanging down the back. The children dressed like the adults. Typically the men shaved, trimmed their beard and cut their hair about three times each year. (Fansler 425)

The streams were alive with trout, and the forests packed with game. Even buffalo could be found in St. George and Holly Meadows at one time. Bear meat and venison were the chief foods. Salt was scarce; it cost a dollar a peck and had to be carried for nearly a hundred miles. Tea was made from catnip and peppermint. Nearly every home had whiskey and brandy. (Fansler 425-426)

John Minear traveled to Moorefield and returned with the irons for one of the first sawmills west of the Allegheny Mountains. Actually, this was a combined sawmill and gristmill. The mill was an up-and-down (sash) sawmill that was equipped as well with corn buhrs for meal grinding. It stood roughly where Elmer Sturm's store was at one time. This location was confirmed in 1875 when a flood on Mill Run washed away a sand bar to reveal the timbers. They were white oak, hewn square, with plainly visible axe marks, well preserved after close to 100 years of immersion. (Fansler 426-427)

New settlers arrived, the settlement prospered, and the colony had nearly doubled its original population by 1794. There were settlers up the river and in Holly Meadows. St. George became the county seat in 1856. "Fort Minear" was the name of the settlement for the first forty years, and "Westernford" was the name for the next forty. And then the state of Virginia ruled that it be named "Saint George." (Fansler 427, 428)

John Minear proved to be a good leader. Minear provided his settlement, as well as the pioneers from other settlements, with a mill to saw their lumber and grind their corn. He also assisted the settlers in the matters of law and the courts and was on such an errand in April 1781, when he was ambushed and killed by Indians. Only a year before, April 1780, his son Jonathan had been massacred by the

Indians. His son, David, was in the service of the Revolutionary War, so leadership of the St. George colony was entrusted to Salathiel Goff. (Fansler 427)

Between 1791 and 1851, not much happened to disturb the life of the colony. Hu Maxwell called it "a silent epoch in our history." However, during this period of sixty years, two events took place that were to change the lives of those living in western Virginia. First, was the building of the Northwestern Turnpike between Winchester and Parkersburg, (1831-1838) that passed through Macomber on Cheat River, eighteen miles below St. George. The second was the building of the Baltimore & Ohio Railway between Cumberland and Wheeling (1850-1852), which passed through Rowlesburg, twenty miles below St. George. The little village of Westernford sprang to life. A movement for a separate county was started. Over the next decade, the town had a new name, a new county, a new state and had endured four years of civil war. (Fansler 428)

William Ewin lived across Cheat River on a 262-acre estate on Clover Run. His home stood near the north end of the Clover Run concrete bridge. The roadway actually passes through his front yard where he displayed the shrubbery and evergreens that he had collected during his travels. A two-story log home was built with a large fireplace in each room. Some time later, a two story addition was added to one end. Most of the furniture was crafted by Ewin, as he was also a cabinetmaker. For some unknown reason, the home was torn down about 1935. William Ewin was an accomplished legislator and lawyer. He represented his district in the Virginia General Assembly prior to the formation of Tucker County. Ewin lobbied for the formation of Tucker County until the legislation cleared the Virginia General Assembly. He was also State Senator in the West Virginia Legislature, serving from 1879 to 1883, when he retired from public life due to cancer. William Ewin passed away on November 25, 1886, and is buried in the family plot just west of the intersection of State Routes 38 and 72 below St. George. (Fansler 433)

The first attempt at establishing a newspaper was in St. George i 1869 by W. Scott Garner of Preston County; he was unsuccessfu Garner returned to Kingwood and created a "Tucker Count Department," in his established newspaper. The *Tucker Count Pioneer* was the first newspaper in St. George, which appeare November 22, 1878; Charles L. Bowman was the publisher. *Th Tucker Democrat* was the second newspaper, which came on Augus 12, 1880, and the publisher was James Porter Scott. An Upshu County native, William M. Cayton, acquired *The Tucker Democrc* on February 14, 1881. Hu Maxwell acquired *The Tucker Count Pioneer* on February 14, 1884. *The Tucker Democrat* moved t Parsons in 1893, when the county seat changed, and it continued t be published until December 28, 1954. *The Tucker County Pionee* gradually declined and ceased publication. *The Tucker Democrc* continued unrivaled in Parsons until William Gustavus Conley cam from Preston County on November 27, 1896, and started *Th Parsons Advocate*. (Fansler 434-435)

The industry of St. George consisted of agriculture, sma sawmills, a shingle mill and a shook mill. The shook mill was bui in 1859. Shook is the name given to a set of staves and heading (ends) for making casks and barrels. Joseph B. Davis and John I Jones rafted thousands of shooks down Cheat River to be freighte out of Rowlesburg. They operated the mill for well over ten yeaı and did much for reviving St. George. The shingle mill was owne by George Auvil and was located on Mill Run about two mile above St. George. (Fansler 381, 435)

Enoch Minear, the son of David Minear and grandson of Joh Minear, lived within and kept a tavern in a stone house that his fathe had built in 1809, along the Limestone road at the edge of town. A that time, a tavern was a lodging house where meals and alcoholi beverages were served. The stone house was also used for earl religious meetings, early school instruction and for jury rooms froı 1856 to 1859. The house stood for eighty-four years but was no used after 1870, when a new house was built. In 1894, it was toı down and the stone used to construct the piers and abutments of th bridge over Cheat River. The stone house was a mansion in its time, and six generations of Minears have lived either in the house or nearby. (Fansler 435-436)

Throughout the first 75 years, there were no schools in St. George. Children were taught the basics, reading, writing and counting, by their parents, if they were accomplished. If not, then the children grew up illiterate. Sometimes, parents employed a tutor to come into their homes and instruct their children. In 1856, at his own expense, Enoch Minear brought the first school to St. George.

He moved an old sawmill from Auvil and rebuilt it as a school near the mouth of Mill Run. George E. Selby was hired to teach the school, and Minear invited children from near and far to attend free of charge. Some walked several miles each way, some boarded in St. George, and others boarded at Minear's Tavern. Public schools came to St. George in 1866, when a two-room school was erected. This school was used until the Board of Education purchased the St. George Academy in 1893. (Fansler 435-436)

St. George was incorporated on April 21, 1880. Town lots had been laid out as early as 1859. The official boundary was as follows: "Beginning at a pin oak on the north side of the road about midway between S.J. Parsons' and H.C. Rosenberger's residences and running thence S 44 ½ W191 poles crossing Cheat river to a rock on the west side of the river, thence N35 W167 poles to another rock near the edge of the river, thence N51 ½ W114 poles to another rock near the edge of the river, near the mouth of Clover run, thence crossing the river N73 E218 poles to a poplar near the Mill Run road, with a large white oak pointer, thence crossing Mill Run S88 E110 poles to a small beech on the west side of a drain near the grave yard on Location road, about one-fourth miles from St. George, thence S7 ½ E to the beginning, containing a little more than one half square miles of territory, to be known as the Town of St. George." (Fansler 429) (Rosenberger lived along the Leadmine road in Dr. Solomon Parsons' old store building)

A fire broke out in December 1888, which heartlessly endangered the town of St. George. Before it could be brought under control, it had consumed three hotels on Main Street, directly across from the courthouse. They were the Blackwater House that was operated by Thomas F. Hebb; the Commercial House that was managed by John A. Shaffer, and the St. George Inn that was run by Martin V. Miller. Carpenter Daniel L. Dumire had built the Saint George Inn in 1859. It was the oldest and best of its kind. Adam Tate managed it for close to twenty years. The Inn's comforts and hospitality were well known throughout the area. Attorneys, cattlemen, and salesmen from surrounding counties and states patronized it. About five years before the fire, Martin V. Miller purchased the inn and renovated it to match any country inn in northern West Virginia. The Talbott House that was managed by William E. Talbott survived the fire. There were two more hotels in St. George by 1890, Hotel Enterprise managed by J. L. Collins, and Shaffer House that was operated by John A. Shaffer. (Fansler 430)

In 1893, the county seat was moved to Parsons and St. George was never able to recover. The Cheat River Railroad Company considered building twenty-six miles of railroad between Rowlesburg and Parsons in 1899, to connect the Baltimore & Ohio and West Virginia Central & Pittsburg Railways. St. George offered the company a free right-of-way and station site in St. George. Parsons feared that if the railroad became a reality, St. George might regain the county seat. (Fansler 401-402, 430)

St. George is the oldest settlement and one of the most enchanting sites in Tucker County today. Golden fields of corn set for harvest, fresh meandering streams, white-tail deer navigating fence lines that border dated farms, friendly folk swathed in mountain culture, one of the most established churches in West Virginia, a stately Academy and various other remnants of another time define this sedate little village tucked along the Cheat that rightly evokes nostalgia.

ST. GEORGE ACADEMY

St. George Academy, an institution of higher learning in Tucker County, became a reality on July 20, 1885, when it was incorporated by John J. Adams, Bascom B. Baker, Ezekiel Harper, William H. Lipscomb, Wilson B. Maxwell, Adam C. Minear, Sansome E. Parsons, and William E. Talbott. They were unable to raise $20,000 by selling stock at $5 per share that was necessary to construct a school building and a dormitory, so a loan was obtained. The first nine months of school was held in the Ann Eliza Church. The second term of school began in the new building in the fall of 1886. (Fansler 437) (Long 333)

For eight years the academy provided classes to meet the requirements of students in all the legal branches of free school study, including physiology. All students were expected to have completed these studies to an extent equivalent to a teacher's certificate of the first grade. Advanced students were prepared for college with rigorous studies in either the Classical Course or the Literary-Scientific course. The Classical Course extended through three years and included Arithmetic, Latin, Greek or German, and Geometry. The Literary-Scientific Course substituted literary and scientific studies for one or both languages. This course included Rhetoric, English Literature, Physical Geography, Trigonometry, Physics, Chemistry, Botany and Astronomy. Special instruction was provided in penmanship and bookkeeping, at a small extra charge. Students could select from the fall, winter or spring terms, or attend the entire year, providing they could pay the tuition: $6 for the short term, $8 for the long term; and Music, $10 for twenty-four lessons. Books were furnished at publisher's prices. Board was provided in public houses from $2 to $3.50 per week and in some private homes at a lower rate. Rooms were also available at DeGraff Hall, located across the street from the academy, and were furnished with a bedstead, mattress, stove, chairs and table for $1 per month. (Fansler 437- 439)

There were two graduating classes from St. George Academy. Graduating in 1889 were Addie Adams, Cora Callihan and Charles Joseph Maxwell. Graduating in 1893 were Anna Tilden Adams and Claude Wilson Maxwell.   (Fansler 437-438)

The Fourth Annual Catalogue of St. George Academy for the term 1888-1889, listed Hattie Parsons, daughter of Solomon J. and Emma Parsons. Hattie was a member of the sophomore class of twenty students. (Fansler 438)

The doors were closed at St. George Academy in June 1893. The St. George District Board of Education purchased the building to be used for a public grade school, and the dormitory, DeGraff Hall, went to private ownership but was later used as a barn and eventually fell into disrepair.   (Fansler 437)

After the new St. George School was completed, the academy was slated for demolition, but the ground floor was repaired and the building was used for another twenty years. In 1982, the building was declared a fire hazard and condemned by the state fire marshal. The Tucker County Board of Education was notified that the academy must be moved or torn down. (Long 333)

St. George and other interested citizens gathered and began making plans to save the academy. The Tucker County Historical Society was enlisted, and in 1984 the Tucker County Board of Education gave the St. George Academy to the historical society with the stipulation that the building be relocated within one year. The group began plans to move the academy. Freda Parsons donated a lot approximately two hundred feet away, and in August 1985 the work began. (Long 333)

The Tucker County Historical Society transferred the title of the St. George Academy to the St. George Preservation Society on June 2, 1988. It is presently used as a historical museum. (Long 335)

Chapter X

WORLEY PARSONS

Worley Parsons and Eva Lena (Metz) Parsons

Married: April 3, 1914
Four children: Margaret (Parsons) Halfin, James Everett, Infant son, and Mary Genevia (Parsons) Gordon

Worley: Born August 22, 1886, Tucker County, West Virginia
Died October 31, 1972, Tucker County, West Virginia

Eva: Born March 27, 1889, Tucker County, West Virginia
Died August 2, 1955, Tucker County, West Virginia

Margaret (Parsons) Halfin: Born February 19, 1916, Tucker County, West Virginia
Died: October 31, 2006, Tucker County, West Virginia

James E. Parsons: Born: February 7, 1918, Tucker County, West Virginia
Died: March 7, 1972, Tucker County, West Virginia

Infant son: Born: December 16, 1920 Died: December 26, 1920

Mary Genevia (Parsons) Gordon: Born March 14, 1924, Tucker County, West Virginia

Worley and Eva Parsons are interred in the St. George Cemetery, St. George, West Virginia.

Worley Parsons is the youngest son of Solomon J. Parsons and Emma (Parsons) Parsons. He was born in Tucker County, West Virginia, on August 22, 1886. Worley is the maternal great-great-grandson of Thomas Parsons Jr. and Mary Rennick. He is also the paternal great-great grandson of Captain James Parsons and Rebecca Simps. Worley Parsons descended from both Parsons brothers.

Worley Parsons married Eva Lena Metz on April 3, 1914, and they are the parents of four children.

Margaret Parsons, the eldest daughter, married Robert Floyd Halfin (1917-1996), and they had two sons, Robert J. and Charles T. Halfin.

James Everett Parsons married Hattie Virginia Oaster (1921-1992), and they had three children, James Marshall, Judith Ann and Mark Allen Parsons.

An infant son was born on December 16, 1920, but the child lived only ten days.

The youngest daughter, Mary Genevia Parsons, married Kenneth L. Gordon (1920-2005) on December 15, 1945. They have three daughters, Carol (Gordon) Carder, Nancy (Gordon) Everson and Christie (Gordon) Allen.

SENIOR CITIZEN WORLEY PARSONS

The Parsons Advocate
Thursday, April 20, 1972

Whether fact or fable, the stories told by this week's Senior Citizen, Worley Parsons, who will be 86 years old on August 22, provide many hours of delightful tales of living in the hills and vales of Tucker County.

Better known to his friends as "Squib," his feats of hunting, fishing and rafting began at an early age. Schooling ended when he was 13 "…when I got too ornery!"

The last surviving member of his immediate family, his three brothers, Marvin, Arthur (Nick), and Prentis, and one sister, Mrs. Hattie Hahn, are deceased. They were the children of the late Solomon J. and Emma (Parsons) Parsons. Both Worley and his parents were lifelong residents of St. George.

Ancestors of a historic family, mention of Worley's father, grandfather and great-grandfather are found in several places in Homer Fansler's "History of Tucker County." The "History of Tucker County" by Hu Maxwell also names Worley's father and mentions his great-grandfather in at least four incidences. The latter history was published in 1884, two years before Worley's birth, but his brothers and sister are named in the edition.

Worley's adventuresome spirit was surely not inherited from any stranger as Fansler's history related that "A few weeks previous to the Confederate raid (August 1862) he (Solomon Parsons) had received a large shipment of merchandise and in a daring display of bravado, sent a taunting message to (Colonel John Daniel) Imboden, daring him 'to come and get it.' To his surprise and chagrin,

Imboden did come and get it. It was quite an achievement for Imboden, but the southern sympathizers in the community soon had to pay dearly for it. In 1863 Parsons moved to Cranberry Summit (Terra Alta) and never resided permanently in Tucker County afterward."

Solomon Parsons' move to what is now known as Terra Alta may have been prompted by the fact that Imboden returned to St. George in November of 1862 and again relieved him of his merchandise. The doctor (a licensed physician) avoided deep snow by wading a river to escape the Confederate soldiers during the second invasion.

Great-grandson Worley has also known many adventures on the rivers in and around St. George. His pursuers were not Confederate soldiers, but conservation officers insisting that he conform to the laws of the day in reference to his hunting and fishing expeditions!

Catching fish was, and still is, one of his favorite sports. Although only able to get around with assistance of his wife and a walker, his first words during the interview were, "I'm going fishing as soon as I can get my pole ready!"

As a youngster he and one of his brothers shot fish with a "plugger" (shotgun), he has gigged them with spears, and he threw back his head and laughed as he told of seining as many as two and three washtubs of suckers and salmon at one time. There was no limit on the number of fish taken, but seining (netting) was illegal so as soon as their seine had dried they hid it each night in a casket at the funeral home. "We knew he'd never think of looking there!"

The urge to go west got him as far as Nebraska but the cold weather drove him home in less than a year. He first worked on a sheep farm helping to feed 5,000 sheep requiring four wagonloads of corn daily. "We had to drive the teams 13 miles to get the corn, we always stopped for a drink before heading home."

Toward spring he went to work "blocking beets" at $20 a month and board, saving his salary until he had enough for train fare back to Grafton where he purchased a bottle of whiskey to keep him company on his walk back to St. George. It was necessary for him to change trains in Chicago and the trip through the city convinced him there was far too much traffic for a country boy and he was glad to be on his way home.

Single until he was 28 years old, he married a schoolmate, Eva Metz, also a native of St. George. They were the parents of four children, two of whom are living. His daughters are Mrs. Robert (Marguerite) Halfin who makes her home in the family homestead in St. George. She has two sons and one grandson. Mrs. Kenny (Mary) Gordon of Philippi has three daughters and one grandson.

One son died in infancy. James Everett Parsons of St. George, the father of three and grandfather of one, died March 7 following a lengthy illness.

Although he made his living in the coalmines and lumber camps he was never afraid declaring he "...didn't have enough sense to be scared." He insisted, "The best place I ever worked in my life," was at a coal mine near Morgantown where he loaded coal for three years and felt hale and hearty.

The only fatal accident he ever witnessed occurred in the woods when a snag from a tree fell on a fellow worker, Joe Dunahugh.
For some time he took contracts for work in the woods, and he commented that he had "...made a lot of money and lost a lot."

Worley Parsons was only seven years old when county courthouse records were stolen in St. George and moved to Parsons, but he vividly remembers that July 1893 event.

Petitions for a vote to relocate the county seat had begun February 12, 1889 and when more than four years had lapsed with no definite preparations in site, those in favor of the move took the matter in their own hands. "Old Man Cayton (William M. Cayton) was county clerk and when he went to Charleston to try to stop them my uncle and cousin and a bunch of men got some wagons and took the records and the bell up to Parsons."

The men returned hungry and tired the next morning only to be refused anything to eat. Worley's mother was angry with them because of their activities. One of Worley's brothers had also tried to get in on the action, but was stopped by his father.

The uncle in question was a favorite of Worley's. He had lost an arm in a logging accident and welcomed the young boy on fishing trips where he could help by baiting his hook. On one occasion Worley remembers helping him drive hogs but when they strayed and wandered into a pond, the young boy only stood and laughed instead of chasing them back onto the path. "He said I '...never did have any sense!' "

Tales of hunting (in season or out) are as numerous as those of his fishing stories. Hunt small game? "I killed more squirrels than a team of horses could haul. I got caught, too, and I paid too! Never had to spend a night in jail though.

"The officer came to the house one day, Said he was wantin' logging grabs' but I knowed better. I was covered with blood from skinnin' a deer but he never did find it."

One of his favorite stories is of the time Lester Miller caught him and Elmer Propst gigging frogs and suckers on the Parson's farm. Worley says the game warden had caught them red-handed with four suckers and seven of the "biggest bull frogs I ever saw" but they managed to open the sack and release their catch before Miller had time to prove anything.

Although "Squib" has never ridden in an airplane, he "... wore out two Model T's and in 1936 I owned a brand new car." During an ox roast at St. George held as a political rally, "...one of those were Old

Abe Helmick always built us a Rt. 72" he had a chance to ride in a touring airplane. "Don't know if I had heart failure or was just tenderhearted," but he turned down the offer.

He and his second wife, the former Lena Lipscomb Barr, live in a small cottage on a road reminiscent of years past. A sign at the entrance to the lane clearly states that snow removal "ends here" and you proceed at your own risk. The desk and tables in the living room were covered with photos of Mr. Parsons's two grandchildren and of Mrs. Parsons's five grandchildren by her former marriage.

Mr. Parsons can hear well, but his vision is badly impaired due to cataracts. His humor is evident and he delights in retelling the stories of his younger days and of old friends, many of them now gone. One childhood friend, Ray Jenkins, still lives in St. George and often visits him and they enjoy reliving the time "Squib" caught a 16-pound salmon and the time he caught "…those two big bass 'that' long!" (The Parsons Advocate, April 1972) This article was printed six months prior to Worley Parsons' death.

EVA (METZ) PARSONS

Eva Lena (Metz) Parsons is the daughter of Jefferson Davis Metz and Amelia Bell (Poling) Metz and was born in Auviltown, below St. George, West Virginia, on March 27, 1889. Jefferson was born on December 28, 1861, in Monongalia County, and he is the son of Elias (1826-) and Minerva (Brookover) Metz. Elias is a son of Peter Metz; they were of German descent. Elias married Minerva, daughter of John Brookover, and they had eleven children. They owned a farm of 294 acres, 150 acres well cultivated, below St George. This was the farm that Jonathan Minear owned when he was killed by the Indians. Elias served with the Union Army during the Civil War. (Maxwell 443)

Jefferson married Amelia Bell Poling on April 24, 1888, and they had nine children: Thomas B. (1888-1967); Everett; William; Eva (Metz) Parsons (1889-1955); Ida (Metz) Arbogast (1893-1977) Theadocie (Metz) Bowman (1901-1965) and Charles who died at eight years of age. Twins Lena and Lula died around three months of age.

Amelia was born November 7, 1868, in Preston County, and is the daughter of Steve and Elizabeth (Dasher) Poling. Jefferson passed away December 1948, and Amelia on August 10, 1950. They are interred in St. George Cemetery, St. George, West Virginia.
(Courtesy of Betty Metz) (Gravesites, St. George Cemetery, St. George, West Virginia)

ST. GEORGE UNITED METHODIST WOMEN

In the fall of 1930, seven women came forward with a common goal, to create the first woman's society of the St. George United Methodist Church. They were Emma Parsons, Eva Parsons, Beatrice Close, Anna Auvil, Flossie Barr, Elva White and Mrs. Westfall. These devoted Christians went door to door soliciting donations and held numerous fundraisers to help maintain the church. Due to a lack of community support and the failing economy, they were forced to disband with the fervent hope that they could regroup at a later date.

Subsequently, on June 30, 1938, a new group formed with the assistance of a new pastor, Reverend Walter Wilmoth. They met bimonthly on the second and fourth Thursday, and the dues were five cents per meeting. The newly-organized "Ladies Aid" helped to clean, support and improve the church. The first officers elected were President, Hazel Miller; Vice President, Leota Loughry; Secretary, Marie Close; and Treasurer, Elvie White. Mrs. Wilmoth and her mother, Mrs. Baker, represented the program committee.

Many dedicated women have served as president to the organization over the past seventy-seven years. They are: Eva Parsons, Dottie White, Lena Sturms, Violet Tennant, Hattie Parsons, Lena Jones and Jane Pifer.

The women's group has assisted the church with many improvements. Projects include interior and exterior painting, tables, chairs, hymnals, carpet, gravel and a new pavilion. A sizeable contribution was made by the society toward the vinyl siding that was purchased in 1991. A new fellowship hall was built in 1995. In September 1997, new shingles were installed to the Sanctuary roof, and vinyl replacement windows were added. A new gas forced-air heating and cooling system was also installed.

The United Methodist Women at St. George United Methodist Church have served their church admirably for well over half a century as janitors, secretaries, teachers and trustees. They have also assisted the community by providing support to those in need.

(Courtesy of St. George United Methodist Church and Gladys Jane Pifer)

DEVOTED PARSONS WOMEN

Emma (Parsons) Parsons, wife of Solomon John Parsons struggled to form the first Ladies Aid during the days of the Great Depression that was kicked off in 1929 by the stock market crash. Emma went door-to-door selling her home-baked goods to raise money for church improvements and the pastor's salary. But those were difficult years during the 1930s, and the society dissolved in spite of her exemplary effort. Emma would have been eighty years of age and widowed in 1930 when the first society formed.

Eva (Metz) Parsons, wife of Worley Parsons, was well known as a soft-spoken Christian lady who embraced deep convictions. At forty-nine years of age, Eva assisted in organizing the Ladies Aid Society in 1938. Like her mother-in-law, Emma Parsons, she worked diligently for the church group. Eva played hostess to many lay speakers who came to the St. George church. They were always welcomed to her comfortable home and good cooking. Eva Parsons was loved and respected by everyone that knew her. Her daughter Mary (Parsons) Gordon, donated a communion service to the church in honor of her mother's service. Eva's name is listed on the memorial plaque that is placed behind the pulpit in the church. The pulpit and altar are believed to have been built by Dr. Solomon Parsons. Eva Parsons was a member of the women's society for seventeen years.

Margaret (Parsons) Halfin, daughter of Eva and Worley Parsons and wife of Robert Halfin, was considered to be an asset to the women's group. Margaret enthusiastically approached each project and willingly donated money and supplies to the church. She was always ready to help. Margaret Halfin was well known for baking her famous donuts. Margaret's name is also listed on the memorial plaque in the church, which commemorates fifty-six years of service.

Hattie (Oaster) Parsons, wife of James Everett Parsons, and daughter-in-law of Eva Parsons, joined the society in 1950. She served as president of the Women's Society of Christian Service from 1969-1977. Hattie also taught the adult Sunday school class and was caretaker of the church for several years. She cleaned the church and prepared for Sunday services. Hattie Parsons served for forty-two years, eagerly participating in projects and church functions.

Freda Parsons is the wife of Maurice Vernon Parsons who is a grandson of Solomon J. Parsons. She has been a member of the women's society since 1955. Freda is well known as a motivator who generated much energy within the group. She cooked at many of the fund raisers and contributed generously. Freda Parsons served as secretary of the group for several years and encouraged Christian women to meet their church-orientated goals for over fifty years. (Courtesy of Gladys Jane Pifer)

St. George United Methodist Church
By Cleta Long

There's a sharp contrast in this church by the road
That entraps a visitor here.
It's not unlike churches I've been in
Yet the difference is strikingly clear.

There's the usual assortment of pews and charts,
Books, and hymnals and scuffmarks of shoes
But a quiet serenity graces the room and
Offers a welcome to you.

And I wonder if maybe, a long time ago,
When the old church was new and quite grand,
The peace was built into it lovingly
Through the labor of gentle hands.

Did they purposely make the doors open wide
And the sanctuary spacious, yet warm
To welcome strangers to enter
And shelter away from life's storms?

Well the church can't talk and tell me
The stories its learned through the years
But I've already gleaned its purpose
And this message comes to my ear.

Saying, "Come sit with me by the side of the road,
We'll let the world go by
And after the rush is over
We'll welcome the weary inside."
(Courtesy of Gladys Jane Pifer and St. George United Methodist Church)

JAMES EVERETT PARSONS

James Everett "Jim" Parsons, the first son of Worley and Eva (Metz) Parsons, was born February 7, 1918, in St. George, West Virginia. He married Hattie Virginia Oaster on July 1, 1941, and they had three children, James Marshall, Judith Ann and Mark Allen.

James was one of seventy-six seniors who graduated from Parsons High School in 1939. Fred Long drove the school bus seventy-seven miles each day and hauled 145 students, forty-two from the St. George area. The first students boarded the bus at 6:30 a.m., and Mr. Long returned from St. George at 5:10 p.m. James played high school football in the position of right half-back for the "Parsons Panthers" under Coach Myel Kepner.
(The Parsons Echo, October 24, 1938)

A Veteran of World War II, James served with the United States Navy from May 2, 1942, to September 21, 1945, and during that service received the Good Conduct Medal. Jim was a member of the Operating Engineers, Local 132, for twenty-five years, and was a business agent for the Union for thirteen years. Following his retirement as business agent, James was employed as equipment foreman by Foster and Wheeler Construction Company at the Harrison County Power Plant at Haywood, near Clarksburg, West Virginia. Parsons served as a superintendent of the Sunday school at St. George United Methodist Church, where he was a member for several years. He was also a member of the Pythagoras Lodge #128 A. F. and A. M. of Parsons and a 32nd Degree Mason in the Valley of the Orient of West Virginia. James Everett Parsons and his wife, Hattie (Oaster) Parsons, are interred in the Parsons Cemetery, Parsons, West Virginia.

238

The Parsons Echo
October 24, 1938

The Football squad of 1938 is larger than that of 1937. There are 30 out this year while last year there were only 23. . .Seniors (are) James Parsons, Virgil Barr, Arthur Barr, Carlton Bennett, Neil Ball, "Chuck" Riley, (and) Mont Wratchford.

The schedule this year carries five home games and four games away. The first encounter was with the Alumni Sept. 10. Next were with Greenbank, Elkins, Terra Alta, and Petersburg. The Panthers have yet to meet Franklin, Keyser, and Belington.

At the opening of the game between Parsons and the Alumni, Arthur Barr broke loose at the kick-off for 90 yards to make a touchdown which was the only scoring of the game that resulted 7-0 in favor of Parsons. Cox made a line plunge which gave the Panthers the extra point. There were approximately 150 to witness the game.

A strong fighting Greenbank Team came to Parsons and defeated the Parsons Panthers 14-6. Fuhrman who was the most outstanding player for the opponents made the two touchdowns and the two extra points to complete the scoring for Greenbank. Cox made the Panthers' only score by a spectacular run for a touchdown.

The Elkins Wimermen defeated Parsons 38-6 under the floodlights in the Wimer stadium before a crowd of five hundred fifty people. The powerful Tigers of Elkins made a score in every quarter except in the last when the hard fighting team of Parsons held them...(Harold) Cox of Parsons got away for a touchdown for the Parsons Panthers who played a hard and a good game though the score ended against them.

Parsons high defeated Terra Alta by a score of 26-7 after a rally in the last half of the game which Terra Alta had the Panthers beaten 7-0 in the first half...(James) Parsons of the Panthers made the first touchdown from the twelve yard line in the third quarter. Riley made the extra point by placement. Cox put over two touchdowns in the fourth quarter and Riley, famous for intercepting passes, grabbed one from the air to make one touchdown, then made the extra point by placement.

Parsons high defeated Petersburg 13-0 at Petersburg. Parsons high made both of its touchdowns in the first quarter. Cox, the star fullback of the Panthers, made both touchdowns. The first from the one yard line in the first two minutes of the game and the other in the latter part of the first quarter in a line plunge from the six-yard line. (Courtesy of Marvin E. Parsons)

The Parsons Echo
November 23, 1938

Parsons Panthers closed their football schedule by defeating Belington 29-6. It was the last football game for seven seniors, "Whitle" Barr, "Chuck" Riley, "Jim" Parsons, Mont Wratchford, "Virg" Barr, "Carty" Bennett, and Neil Ball. Parsons won six games and lost three.

Cox scored in the first two minutes from the six yard line after Belington fumbled on the Parsons 25 yard line. Cox in the first quarter again got the ball and ran 48 yards to score for the Panthers. A. Barr converted for both extra points by placement. There was no more scoring until the last quarter when Cox carried the ball for another touchdown. Belington scored in the last few minutes of the game. (Courtesy of Marvin E. Parsons)

We Shall Live Again

By Mrs. Meade Gutshall

Death is only a dream
To those who die in Him,
We have the Blessed Assurance
That we shall live again.

If we are true and faithful
And serve Him as we live,
A beautiful mansion will await us
That sweet promise Christ did give.
And tho' our time on earth be brief
As was the life of him –departing,
Up in Heaven we shall live on
Up there life will just be starting.

"Jim" was true to God and loved ones
Doing his best along the way,
And now he is "asleep in Jesus"
We'll meet him again some happy day.

He bore his suffering with a smile
He knew the Lord was always near,
And he faced what e'er befell him
Without doubts and without fear.

Those left behind, must look to Jesus
He knows all your secret grief,
He alone can give you comfort
He can give you sweet relief.

Up in Heaven beyond life's sorrows
All our loved ones we shall meet,
Where we shall know no more sadness
And the family circle will be complete
(Written at the passing of James E. Parsons in 1972)

HATTIE (OASTER) PARSONS

Hattie Virginia (Oaster) Parsons was the daughter of Isaac H. and Nora B. (Moats) Oaster and was born at Philippi, West Virginia, on July 4, 1921. She had two brothers, Bernard and Melvin, and three sisters, Ruth (Oaster) Tennant, Mary (Oaster) Bodkin and Minnie (Oaster) Heckel.

Bran flakes cost nine cents a box when Hattie's father, Isaac Oaster, had a grocery store on the corner of First and Water streets in Parsons in the early 1930s. Isaac and Nora Oaster, natives of Barbour County, came to Parsons in 1920 when he went to work at the Pulp Mill. Isaac was employed by the A&P Store and later, at Bennett Department Store, until it was destroyed by fire. Isaac Oaster then opened his own establishment, where he remained about six years before opening a small store in the Pulp Mill Bottom, in the home that last belonged to Dorman and Dorothy Carr. That home was struck by the flood of 1985 and has since been demolished.

Hattie Parsons was a member of the St. George United Methodist Church and the Women's Society in Christian Service. She also served as past matron with the Order of Eastern Star Lodge No. 91, Parsons Chapter. She graduated from Parsons High School in 1939, where she was an honors graduate. Hattie passed away on November 12, 1992, in the Davis Memorial Hospital, Elkins, West Virginia, following a brief illness.

SOLOMON JOHN PARSONS HOUSE

Many Parsons "mansions of the day" once graced Tucker County. Certainly not a mansion but quite splendid in its prime, the three-story white farmhouse embraces the Leadmine road, a meager one-half mile east of the small village of St. George, West Virginia. Mary (Parsons) Gordon, who lived most of her young life on the Parsons farm, believes that the farmhouse was built about 1891, when her father, Worley "Squib" Parsons, was five years of age. It is presently recognized as the Solomon J. Parsons House.

In his will of 1811, Captain James Parsons granted to his sons Isaac, Dr. Solomon and Jonathan his lands on the Cheat River, known as the Horseshoe Bottom. The division and boundaries had previously been agreed upon by the father and sons. Maxwell tells us that James Parsons had divided the land, which he acquired in the Horseshoe, among his sons about the time he had obtained the deeds. Dr. Solomon Parsons was allotted the farm on or near the site of the first fort built by Minear's colony on the county farm. (93)

Dr. Solomon's son, James William Parsons, inherited the county farm land. His home "stood on a bluff overlooking the Cheat River..." In 1860, James W. Parsons retired from business, divided his lands among his children and moved to Kingwood, West Virginia. Sansome Elliott Parsons inherited his father's farm. (MacCabe 242-243)

James W. Parsons granted to his son, Solomon John, two tracts of land. The first tract was for 147¼ acres "being the tract on which the grantee now resides; it being the upper end of the old Salathiel Goff survey of 250 acres on the east side of Cheat River and at the mouth of Dry Run." It is believed that the home where Solomon J. Parsons resided in 1873 was located behind the present-day St. George farmhouse and that some time prior to 1891 the home was destroyed by fire. When Solomon John received the land from his father, he was twenty-five years of age and had been married four years. At that time, he and Emma had two children, three-year-old Prentice and Hattie, seven months of age.

According to Fansler, Dr. Solomon Parsons' home and store were located where the St. George-Leadmine road crosses Lower Dry Run, a half-mile east of St. George. He goes on to say that the property descended through his son, James William, to his grandson, Solomon John, and to his great-grandson, Worley. Although we are uncertain as to the exact location of the home and store, I believe that Solomon John Parsons was residing in the home of his grandfather, Dr. Solomon Parsons, when he was deeded the Parsons farm in 1873. (196)

When the boundaries were established for the town of St. George by surveyor John D. Nestor in February 1880, it began at a pin oak on the north side of the road about midway between Solomon John Parsons' and H.C. Rosenberger's residences. Fansler tells us that Rosenberger and his wife, Hannah, lived along the Leadmine road, in Solomon Parsons' old store building that was later torn down. (431)

Salathiel Goff accompanied the party of pioneers who traveled from the South Branch in Hardy County to Tucker County (Augusta County, Virginia) with John Minear in March 1774, and again in 1776. Goff acquired two tracts of land, one being a 250-acre tract just east of St. George where Woodrow Nestor resided. This tract bordered Solomon J. Parsons' land. Salathiel Goff died June 27, 1791, in St. George. The Indians were on the warpath at that time, so Goff was hurriedly buried at his request under a hickory tree on his St. George farm. The grave is approximately one hundred feet from the front door of the present-day home of Mr. and Mrs. James Flanagan. (Fansler 54, 55, 62)

Daniel L. Dumire was a master carpenter in the St. George area. Dumire was born in 1834 and would have been fifty-seven years of age about the time the Parsons farmhouse was built. We know that he built the Saint George Inn and the Methodist Episcopal Church South in 1859, at age twenty-five. But it is uncertain who built the Parsons farmhouse.

The three-story farmhouse was expertly framed with pine timber that was cut on the Parsons farm. Beneath the present-day vinyl siding, one can readily identify the original German lap siding. Stone slabs, two-feet wide and one-foot in depth, were retrieved from the banks of Mill Run to create a solid foundation. The house had two brick chimneys, and each of the rooms had flues that accessed one of the chimneys. The kitchen flue provided ventilation for the wood-fired cook stove, and a solitary brick fireplace graced the front parlor. All the brick used in the farmhouse was molded and fired on the Parsons farm.

Eight spacious rooms were decked with lathe and plastered walls, red oak hardwood floors and ornate oak base and window trim. Fine-looking oak and walnut wainscoting adorned the kitchen and dining room. The dwelling has a large third-floor attic and a cellar beneath one-half the house. It was truly a fine home in its time.

Over the past one hundred years, the major improvements to the farmhouse included vinyl replacement windows, a large front porch that extends the width of the house and a third-floor dormer. A screened-in back porch was remodeled into a bathroom and small vestibule.

Unfortunately, the house and farm fell into gradual disrepair over the past fifty years. In June 2004, the farmhouse was purchased by Mr. and Mrs. James M. Parsons, a great-grandson of Solomon John Parsons, and restoration began straight away. But sadly, the farm that once thrived along the Cheat River bottom has vanished. Those treasured warm summer days with dogs barking, the hum of hay bailers in the fields below, and the sweet aroma of pies baking in Grandma Parsons' kitchen can not be resurrected.

Countless friends and neighbors have crossed the threshold of the Parsons farmhouse. Many soft and several calloused hands have grasped the handrail of the dark oak stairway that ascends to the second floor, and various youngsters have straddled that very banister and swiftly descended to the first floor.

Everyone was warmly welcomed to the Parsons homestead and made comfortable, regardless of the length of stay. They slept on soft warm beds, beneath hand-stitched quilts, dined on the best cooking for miles around, worked alongside the family, fished in the Cheat River, and hunted white-tail deer in the surrounding fields and mountains. Emma Parsons' parents, Job Parsons Sr. and Sarah (Losh) Parsons, spent their waning years at her St. George home. Moreover, Eva Parsons' parents, Jeffery and Amelia Metz, spent their declining years in the home and each passed away there.

Solomon Parsons was granted a second tract of land from his father that amounted to 252 acres, which joined the first tract. In his will dated April 1925, Solomon bequeathed to his son Worley Parsons all real estate, including the home farm and the adjacent upland, during the period of his natural life, with the remainder to Worley's children. He gave Emma one-half his interests in all livestock and farm machinery, implements and utensils, owned jointly by Worley and Solomon. Solomon had previously granted around eighty-two acres to his son Marvin.

When Solomon J. Parsons passed away on December 10, 1926, at seventy-eight years of age, Worley was forty years old and had been married to Eva for twelve years. They had three children, Margaret, James, and Mary; an infant son had lived only ten days.

Solomon Parsons and his youngest son, Worley, farmed the land that was passed down from their fathers and grandfathers. It is well known that the farmer is devoted to the land and must adhere to a vital routine that is necessary to care for the livestock, cultivate the fields and gardens, prepare and preserve the food and sell the bounty. And, so it was with the Parsons farm.

At daybreak, Worley Parsons hurried to the barn that was a shor distance below the farmhouse to milk several cows. He promptly brought the milk to Eva who separated it into "blue John" and cream in the small pantry adjacent to the kitchen. The cream was late collected by the postman and carried eight miles to Parsons for sale The skim milk, along with leftovers, was carted to the hog lot and fed to at least a dozen greedy pigs and piglets. Eva also sold creamy cottage cheese and fresh eggs to help raise funds for the farm. Folks came from near and far to buy her fare.

Eva Parsons cooked three large meals each day on the wood-fired kitchen stove that warmed the kitchen and adjoining rooms. The bulky black iron stove set in the hub of the farmhouse kitchen, where she prepared a breakfast of cured ham and bacon, eggs that had been gathered from the chicken house, oatmeal, pancakes, home-canned jelly and jam, prepared from grapes and berries grown on the farm freshly-baked bread, coffee and tea. Eva preferred brewed tea, and Worley preferred coffee "sopped" with homemade bread.

Afterwards, Worley went off to the fields for a full day's work From early dawn until dusk he repaired or built new fence, sowed oats and corn in the spring, and made hay during the summer months. Animals on the farm, like the young calves, were cared for daily, much like a small child who requires nurturing from infancy to maturity.

The "hog lot" bordered the farmhouse. Here, on approximately three acres of rocky hillside, Worley kept several hogs that were butchered for the family, more often around the holidays. Hams and front shoulders were cured, sausage was prepared, and soap was made from the lard. On occasion, a number of the animals were carried to the stock sale or sold to neighboring farmers.

Eva Parsons was an ardent gardener. She loved flowers and grew a variety of multicolored blossoms in a small garden near the front porch of the farmhouse. She winterized many of her plants in the front setting room where they thrived in the subdued light and cool environment.   Worley and Eva also had a large vegetable garden below the farmhouse, and a "truck patch" in the lower bottom, where they grew produce in abundance for preservation, which included green beans, corn, beets, asparagus, tomatoes, squash, carrots, onions, peppers, peas, potatoes, and lots of pumpkins. Eva canned her own pumpkin; she was celebrated for her mouth-watering pumpkin pies.

Following the noon meal that Eva served promptly at twelve o'clock, Worley took a short, well-deserved nap, before returning to the fields. After the five o'clock meal, he returned once more to the fields and worked until darkness closed in.   But on rare warm summer evenings, when the day's chores were completed, Worley headed across the lower bottom to the Cheat River with his fishing pole and carbide light to "sucker fish." He loved to fish, but occasionally, he would saunter the half-mile into St. George to Elmer Sturms's store that sold groceries and Gulf gasoline and sit around with his neighbors on the chatting bench, chewing tobacco and telling ghost stories.

For several years Eva read her Bible each night and Jim completed his homework by an oil lamp.   After electricity was installed in the farmhouse, Worley huddled close to the radio each evening and, from his easy chair, listened to Lowell Thomas. With his standard opening, "Good evening, everybody," Lowell Thomas brought news and a sense of adventure from remote sites around the world into America's living rooms.   Frequently, the entire family gathered for snacks; a favorite was canned tomatoes and oyster crackers.

Eva stored the brown sugar in a sealed canister in the lower kitchen cupboard, and when Mother wasn't looking, Mary and Margaret would snitch a piece of the sweetie. When the girls wanted Eva to make candy, they cajoled Jim into asking their mother. Mary remembers that "Mom would do just about anything for Jim."

Each Sunday following the church services, the farmhouse and front porch swelled to overflowing. Eva Parsons' home was the gathering place for family and friends. The Jim Parsons family came, Jim and Hattie, and children, Marshall and Judy. The Gordon's came too: Kenny, Mary and children, Carol Lynn and Nancy. Now and then, the Halfin's came by: Bob, Margaret and sons, Joe and Tom. And Eva's extended family came too: her sister and brother-in-law, Theadocie or "Docia" as they called her, and Raymond Bowman. Many summers the Bowmans came for weeks at a time and camped in the lower bottom. Eva was always a gracious hostess; the dining room table was laden with platters and bowls of favorite foods. Friends and family cherished Eva's Sunday dinner, and they visited until dusk.

A large wormy chestnut, two-story barn stood below the house in the farm yard along with a corncrib, chicken house, silo, and smokehouse. Near the backside of the farmhouse was a two-story granary. Beans and onions were dried in the top of the building and a small creek flowed beneath the structure that cooled the cream. Farm equipment in those days included an International Farmall tractor, plows and disk, hay baler, hay tetter, hay rake, conveyor that carried hay to the barn, corn seeder, cultivators, mowing machine, and manure spreader.

Timber grew abundantly on the Parsons farm: walnut, sycamore, locus, hickory, cherry, oak, and a few maple trees. A large apple orchard covered a lower bottom and peach trees grew plentifully. Eva spent hours cracking out walnuts and hickory nuts for cookies and candy. The purple and white grape harbors flourished, and people came for miles around to buy bushels of grapes.

Eva was exemplary in her Christian principles. She was a loving mother and grandmother who was deeply devoted to her family and neighbors. She was known to share her produce and preserved food with any needy person and often sent Worley with foodstuff to help others. Eva Parsons' sincere devotion extended to her church as well. She worked diligently for the St. George United Methodist Church and Ladies Aid Society and regularly attended the Methodist conference and sought pastors for the church. She labored even more diligently to help pay their salaries.

Eva Parsons succumbed to cancer on August 2, 1955, in the Broaddus Hospital, Philippi, West Virginia, where she had been a patient for five weeks. Services were conducted at the St. George Methodist Church in St. George, West Virginia, by Reverend Howard McNeill and her dear friend, Reverend Mrs. Sadie Triplett, a Methodist minister of Cumberland, Maryland. Reverend Triplett and Mrs. Starkey were traveling evangelists who often stayed over at Eva Parsons' home while holding revivals in the area. Worley was eighty-six years of age when he passed away on November 2, 1972, following an extended illness.

Since the time the land was deeded to Solomon John Parsons in 1873, five generations have resided on the Parsons farm: (1) Solomon J. and Emma (Parsons) Parsons; (2) Worley and Eva (Metz) Parsons; (3) James E. and Hattie (Oaster) Parsons; Kenneth and Mary (Parsons) Gordon; Robert and Margaret (Parsons) Halfin; (4) Mark and Charlotte (Bartlett) Parsons; James M. and Darlene (Irvin) Parsons; and (5) David M. and Melinda (Sherman) Parsons.

Two hundred and forty-five years ago, Captain James Parsons was captured by the Indians and carried to Ohio where he later escaped. Attempting to return to his home on the South Branch of the Potomac, in present-day Hardy County, Captain Parsons discovered virgin country, land that revealed such vast beauty in summer and even more breathtaking splendor in the autumn. He had discovered Tucker County, West Virginia. From his timely exploration came the pioneers who settled the mountainous countryside nestled along the Cheat River.

The End

Bibliography

Bosworth, Dr. A.S. 1975. *History of Randolph County.* Parsons, WV: McClain Printing Company.

Driver, Robert J. 1988. *14th Virginia Cavalry.* Lynchburg, VA: Howard.

Fansler, Homer Floyd. 1962. *History of Tucker County West Virginia.* Parsons, WV: McClain Printing Company.

Genealogical Society of Utah. 1936. Salt Lake City, Utah: Desert Book Company.

Long, Cleta M. 1996. *History of Tucker County West Virginia.* Parsons, WV: McClain Printing Company.

Maxwell, Hu. 1884. *History of Tucker County, West Virginia.* Kingwood, WV: Preston Publishing Company.

Maxwell, Hu. 1991. *History of Randolph County.* Parsons, WV: McClain Printing Company.

Maxwell, Hu and Swisher, H.L. 1990. *History of Hampshire County.* Parsons, WV: McClain Printing Company.

MacCabe, Virginia Parsons. 1913. *Parsons Family History and Record.* Decatur Illinois: Charles W. Nickey.

MacMaster, Richard K. *The History of Hardy County 1786-1986.* Salem, WV: Walsworth Press, Inc. Regional director: Don Mills, Inc.

Moore, Commander Alvin Edward. 1963. *History of Hardy County of the Borderland.*

Moorefield Examiner and Hardy County News. Moorefield, West Virginia.

West Virginia Archives and History Website. Accessed online at www.wvculture.com